Indiana

Indiana

Ann Heinrichs

Children's Press®
A Division of Grolier Publishing
New York   London   Hong Kong   Sydney
Danbury, Connecticut

Frontispiece: Snow along Little Elkhart River

Front cover: The Gold Dome, Notre Dame

Back cover: A farm near Edinburg

Consultant: Andrea Bean Hough, senior subject specialist, Indiana Division, Indiana State Library

Please note: All statistics are as up-to-date as possible at the time of publication.

Visit Children's Press on the Internet at http://publishing.grolier.com

Book production by Editorial Directions, Inc.

Library of Congress Cataloging-in-Publication Data

Heinrichs, Ann.
    Indiana / Ann Heinrichs.
      144 p. 24 cm. — (America the beautiful. Second series)
    Includes bibliographical references and index.
    Summary : Describes the geography, plants, animals, history, economy, language, religions, culture, sports, arts, and people of the state of Indiana.
    ISBN 0-516-21038-6
    1. Indiana Juvenile literature. [1. Indiana.] I. Title. II. Series.
F526.3H45 2000
977.2—dc21
                                    98-35218
                                          CIP
                                          AC

Acknowledgments

For their kind assistance in this project, I am grateful to innumerable employees of Indiana's state information center, tourism department, historical society, and historical bureau; and to all the Hoosiers who shared their homes and experiences with me.

Clifty Falls

Downtown Indianapolis

Lincoln's boyhood home

Contents

Trumpeter swan

Hoosiers

Lake Michigan

The Indy 500

A peony

CHAPTER ONE

A State Built on Traditions

We reached our new home about the time the state came into the Union. It was a wild region, with many bears and other wild animals still in the woods. There I grew up. There were some schools, so called; but no qualification was ever required of a teacher beyond 'readin', writin', and cipherin'."

He was just eight years old when he and his parents left Kentucky to settle in southern Indiana's Spencer County. Strong and good with an axe, he cleared acres of dense forest, chopped firewood, and split logs into rails for fences.

Abraham Lincoln reading by firelight

There was little time for school, and his formal education totaled only about one year. But the young man loved to read, and many nights found him stretched out in front of the fireplace with a book. Some of his favorites were the Bible, *Aesop's Fables,* and *The Adventures of Robinson Crusoe.* In time, he became a brilliant lawyer—and the sixteenth president of the United States. His name was Abraham Lincoln.

Growing up on the Indiana frontier was rough when Abe was a boy. Many children, like Abe, had to spend more time working than going to school. Schools—where there *were* any—were simple, one-room log cabins in the wilderness. Parents pitched in to build them and found schoolmasters to teach there. They paid the teacher a certain amount per child and took turns feeding and housing him or her.

Opposite: A covered bridge in Cataract Falls State Park

Many years ago, schools had only one room, and students sat on long, hard benches.

For teachers and students alike, just getting to school was a challenge. Many had to walk miles through rain or snow, only to sit shivering on log benches in the dim and drafty schoolhouse.

Schools in Spencer County have changed quite a bit since Abe's time. Now they close when the snow is too deep for travel, and snow make-up days are added at the end of the year. Students are designing their own Internet websites—something Abe could never have imagined as he read by the flickering firelight. Instead of chopping firewood, today's young people get their exercise play-

Geopolitical map of Indiana

Today's schools are much different from in Lincoln's time. Students have individual desks, computers, and other modern equipment.

ing basketball, football, and tennis. While Abe cleared trees, at least one class now holds a tree-planting day.

By now, almost every aspect of life has changed for Hoosiers, as Indiana residents are called. Indiana is one of the most indus-

Why Hoosiers?

People in Indiana are called Hoosiers, and Indiana is known as the Hoosier State. The term first appeared in the 1830s, but no one seems to know exactly where it comes from. These are some of the most popular theories:

When a visitor knocked on an Indiana settler's door, the settler would ask, "Who's yere?" — which sounded like "Hoosier."

Indiana rivermen often got into fistfights and beat up, or "hushed," their opponents. The rivermen were known as "hushers" — which became "Hoosiers."

According to Indiana native James Whitcomb Riley, Indiana backwoodsmen got into vicious fights, sometimes even biting off a nose or an ear in a barroom brawl. When someone later spotted an ear on the floor, they would ask, "Whose ear?" — which became "Hoosier."

Which theory is the right one? Take your pick! ▪

trialized states in the nation. It exports steel, chemicals, and machinery to countries all over the world. A trip that took hours in the old days takes just a few minutes today.

Still, it's surprising how much has stayed the same. Even today, almost three-fourths of the state is farmland. Drive just beyond any big city, and endless acres of fields stretch before your eyes.

Traditional values are still very much alive too. Hard work and self-reliance have been part of Indiana's heritage since its earliest days. And that's how Hoosiers built their frontier wilderness into the industrial giant it is today.

Children in Indiana get their exercise in many ways, including playing sports such as soccer.

CHAPTER TWO

Out of the Wilderness

LOSSING=BARRITT

ndiana's earliest known people belonged to what is called Mississippian culture. They lived in scattered villages along the Ohio River, where they built earthen forts and burial mounds. Because they left behind huge, beehive-shaped mounds of earth, they're often called the Mound Builders.

The most famous mound site in Indiana is Angel Mounds, near Evansville. This settlement was once the largest city in what is now Indiana. Several thousand people lived there. They survived by hunting and farming, and a community grew up for miles around the town.

Angel Mounds is now a historic site near Evansville.

Opposite: General Anthony Wayne defeating the Miami Indians at the Battle of Fallen Timbers

Angel Mounds State Historic Site

People of the Mississippian culture lived on the banks of the Ohio in southwestern Indiana from 1100 to 1450. A village they built near present-day Evansville is now called Angel Mounds. The town was a chiefdom—the home of a chief—protected by a stockade made of tree branches and mud. Like other Mississippian people, the residents built large earthen mounds. No one knows why the people deserted the village. The site is named after Mathias Angel and his descendants, who once owned the land. ■

Some of their mounds were temples, where priests carried out ceremonies and rituals. On other mounds, upper-class families built their homes. Still others were meeting places or garbage dumps. By around 1450, the once-thriving culture at Angel Mounds had disappeared. Scattered Mississippian settlements still survived along the Ohio River until the early 1600s.

In the years to come, many other Indian groups occupied Indiana. They included the Miami, Potawatomi, Delaware, Kickapoo, and Shawnee. Some groups banded together for hunting, warfare, or mutual protection from other groups. Algonquin Indians, for example, persuaded several other tribes to join them in forming the Miami Confederacy as protection from the warlike Iroquois Confederacy.

As white settlers moved onto lands along North America's East Coast, they pushed the Indians farther west. Thus, many of Indiana's native people were originally eastern tribes. One by one, these groups, too, either sold their land to white settlers or were driven out.

Explorers and Settlers

The first European to set foot in present-day Indiana was the French explorer René-Robert Cavelier, Sieur de La Salle. He arrived in 1679, sailing from the French colonies in Canada through Michigan and on to Indiana's St. Joseph River. La Salle was hoping to find a way to sail all the way to the Pacific Ocean and claim the surrounding lands for France. Although he fell short of his goal, he explored much of northern Indiana.

French fur traders and Jesuit missionaries were the next to arrive. The traders set up trading posts in the 1720s, where they gave the Indians beads, blankets, and whiskey in exchange for furs. Two important posts were Fort Miami (now Fort Wayne) and

The Native Americans who inhabited the plains were eventually driven out by the white settlers.

René-Robert Cavelier, Sieur de La Salle

Fort Ouiatenon (near Lafayette). Jesuit missionaries founded the settlement of Vincennes around 1732. It became the largest and most important town in the territory and its first permanent settlement.

Meanwhile, English colonists from the East Coast were pushing deeper into the western frontier. In their minds, they had the right to all the territory west of their coastal colonies. Both the British and the French kept building forts on the frontier, and hostilities broke out from time to time.

It was probably inevitable that these conflicts exploded into an all-out war. It began in 1754 and was called the French and Indian War, although it was really between France and Britain. American Indians were deeply

Jesuit missionaries founded settlements throughout Indiana.

involved, however, and both sides used Indians to help them fight the war.

In 1763, England and France finally made peace in the Treaty of Paris. France gave Britain most of its land east of the Mississippi River, including what is now Indiana. To keep a firm grip on their new territories, the British built forts throughout the region. One British stronghold was Fort Sackville, built in 1763 in Vincennes.

The American Revolution

The peace did not last long, though. Sick of foreign rule and foreign taxes, the American colonies went to war with Britain to gain their independence. When the American Revolution broke out in 1775, settlers rallied to the cause and took up arms to fight for their freedom.

George Rogers Clark fought in Indiana during the American Revolution.

A Virginia officer named George Rogers Clark marched into Indiana with his troops in 1778 and won Fort Sackville from the British. The British recaptured the fort, so Clark retreated and rallied his men for another try. In the bitter winter of 1779, Clark's troops began their march from Kaskaskia, Illinois. At last, on February 25, 1779, the Americans defeated the British and took Fort Sackville and Vincennes. With this victory, present-day Indiana became American soil. In the Treaty of Paris of 1783, which

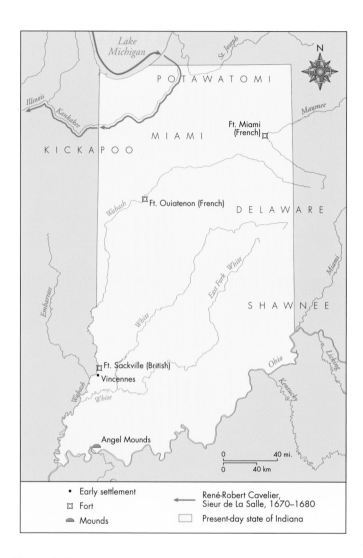

Exploration of Indiana

formally ended the American Revolution, Great Britain officially gave this land to the United States.

The Northwest Territories

The new nation now faced the problem of governing the vast frontier north and west of the Ohio River. Congress passed the Northwest Ordinance on July 13, 1787. This law established the Northwest Territory—which included what is now Indiana, as well as Ohio, Michigan, Illinois, Wisconsin, and part of Minnesota.

The ordinance granted many of the freedoms that Americans had fought and died for in the American Revolution. At the top of the list were freedom of religion and the right to a trial by jury. No citizen in the territory was to be punished cruelly for crimes or to be imprisoned or have property taken without a trial.

Later, in 1791, the U.S. Bill of Rights gave religious and civil liberties to white male citizens. But the Northwest Ordinance had granted these rights four years earlier. There was to be no slavery in the Northwest Territory, although some people got around the law by keeping unpaid African-American "servants."

The rights of Native Americans were supposed to be honored too, but that provision collapsed fairly easily as more and more settlers moved in. Battles between whites and Indians broke out on a regular basis. One persistent group was the Miami, led by Chief Little Turtle, who often raided Indiana farms and villages. Finally the federal government sent in General Anthony Wayne, nicknamed "Mad Anthony." In 1794, he defeated the Indians in the Battle

Chief Little Turtle was the leader of the Miami tribe in the 1790s.

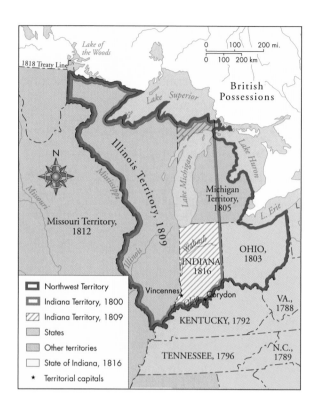

Map labels:
- Lake of the Woods
- 1818 Treaty Line
- British Possessions
- Lake Superior
- Lake Michigan
- Lake Huron
- L. Erie
- Illinois Territory, 1809
- Missouri
- Mississippi
- Michigan Territory, 1805
- Missouri Territory, 1812
- Illinois
- Wabash
- OHIO, 1803
- INDIANA 1816
- Vincennes
- Corydon
- Ohio
- VA., 1788
- KENTUCKY, 1792
- N.C., 1789
- TENNESSEE, 1796

Legend:
- Northwest Territory
- Indiana Territory, 1800
- Indiana Territory, 1809
- States
- Other territories
- State of Indiana, 1816
- ★ Territorial capitals

Scale: 0 100 200 mi. / 0 100 200 km

Historical map of Indiana

of Fallen Timbers, a site along the Maumee River near present-day Toledo, Ohio. In the treaty that followed, Indians agreed to a peace and granted large tracts of land for white settlement.

Plans for new states were also part of the Northwest Ordinance. The Northwest Territory could be broken into three to five states, but first a region had to become an official territory. Indiana Territory was established in 1800. It consisted of almost all of the Northwest Territory, except present-day Ohio and a part of Michigan. Vincennes was the capital city, and William Henry Harrison became the first territorial governor. Ohio, the first state to be

Tecumseh and the Prophet

Tecumseh (1768?–1813) was born in what is now Ohio, the son of a Shawnee chief and a Creek-Cherokee woman. In 1805, Tecumseh's brother Tenskwatawa (right), called the Shawnee Prophet (1768–1834), began preaching to various groups of Indians. Tecumseh took this chance to organize resistance against white settlers. The Prophet clashed with General William Henry Harrison in the 1811 Battle of Tippecanoe. Tecumseh was killed in the Battle of the Thames in 1813. ■

formed from the Northwest Territory, joined the Union as the seventeenth state in 1803.

Indiana Territory's boundaries changed a little over the next few years. It lost some land when Michigan Territory was formed in 1805 and Illinois Territory in 1809.

The Last of the Indian Wars

Many Indians had never accepted losing their homelands to the whites in unfair treaties. Shawnee chief Tecumseh and his brother, called the Shawnee Prophet, began rallying the Indians again to resist white settlement in Canada and the Northwest Territory. This time, the conflict came to a head at the Battle of Tippecanoe, near Lafayette.

General William Henry Harrison marched his troops into Indian Territory in 1811. As the troops camped on Tippecanoe Creek, the Prophet led a surprise attack, and Harrison's men fought them off. Harrison became a hero and acquired the nickname "Old Tippecanoe," or just "Old Tip" for short.

General William Henry Harrison battles Tecumseh.

Harrison fought the Indians again at the Battle of the Thames in 1813 in Canada. These victories put an end to Indian resistance—not only in Indiana, but throughout the Northwest Territory.

Statehood at Last

In 1813, Indiana Territory moved its capital from Vincennes to Corydon, in Harrison County. Delegates met there for a constitutional convention in 1816. They drew up a constitution and sent it to the U.S. Congress for approval.

The great day came at last. On December 11, 1816, President James Madison signed Congress's resolution for Indiana statehood, making Indiana the nineteenth state to join the Union. Its borders were drawn once and for all, just as they are today. Corydon was declared the state capital, and voters elected Jonathan Jennings as their first governor. (Today, the old capitol in Corydon is a state historic site.)

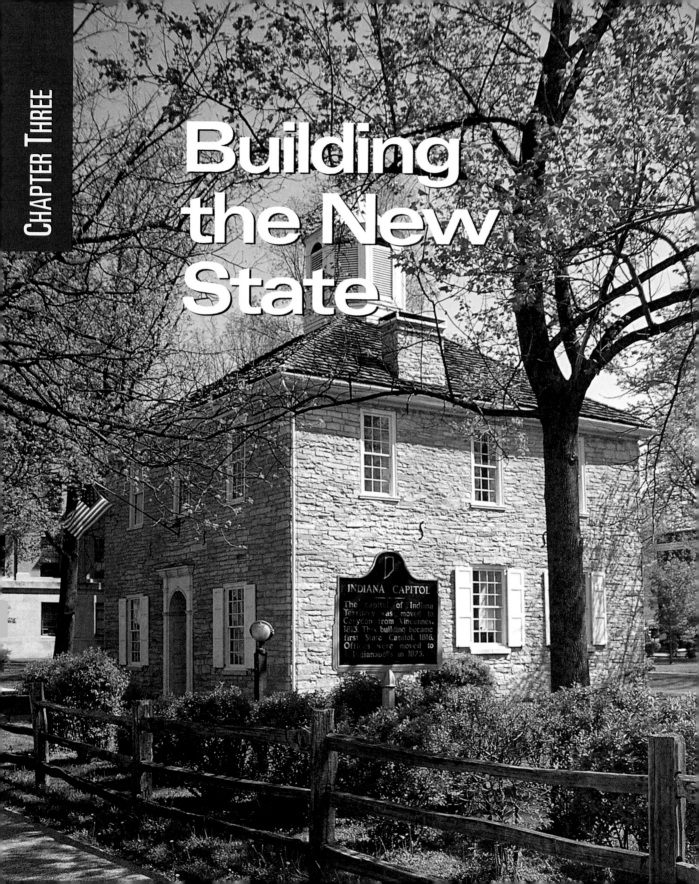

CHAPTER THREE

Building the New State

INDIANA CAPITOL

The capital of Indiana Territory was moved to Corydon from Vincennes, 1813. This building became first State Capitol, 1816. Offices were moved to Indianapolis in 1825.

At the time of statehood, most of Indiana was still a wilderness. Pioneers settled in the southern part of the state, along the Ohio River—just as Indians had done many centuries before. Settlers arrived from the south and east in rickety wagons loaded down with household goods. Others came on horseback or even on foot. They bought land from the federal government and cleared the dense forest for their farms.

Because there were no stores, pioneers had to grow or make whatever they needed. At first, people made clothing from animal skins. Later they made their clothes from homespun cotton and wool cloth. Women knitted warm caps for winter and sewed sunbonnets for summer. In winter, homemade leather shoes protected their feet, but in summer, it was easiest for everyone just to go barefoot.

Many settlers traveled the Ohio River on their way to a new life in Indiana.

Opposite: The first state capitol in Corydon

One of these early settlers became one of the United States' greatest leaders. Thomas and Nancy Lincoln left Kentucky in 1816 to settle in southern Indiana's Spencer County. Their son, Abe, was only eight years old. He worked all day, but he loved reading so much that he read even while he plowed the fields. Abe lived in Indiana till he was twenty-one years old.

Young Abraham Lincoln chopped wood and did many other chores.

"Ideal" Communities

Another Indiana settler was George Rapp. This German religious leader founded a group called the Harmony Society, or Harmonists. Its members worked for the welfare of the group, and all goods were common property. In 1814, Rapp and the Harmonists bought land along the Wabash River in Posey County and set up a community called Harmony. It wasn't easy. There were dense forests to clear, swamps to drain, and houses to build. Although their neighbors did not approve of them, the Harmonist community flourished for ten years. They tended their vineyards, flocks of sheep, and herds of cattle. They lived in sturdy homes of brick and stone, and they made their own clothes.

When Rapp decided to move his people to Pennsylvania, he sold the land to a Scottish industrialist named Robert Owen. When

Owen founded New Harmony in 1825, he too had visions of an ideal society. He organized a communal settlement of scholars, scientists, and teachers who believed in his bold new ideas about getting rid of poverty and competition. The revolutionary ideals of New Harmony even attracted foreign leaders, who visited to listen and learn.

Owen's grand plan required members to be supremely unselfish and to respect others' rights—a tall order for any society! His community failed after only two years, but his ideas inspired later movements, such as for women's rights and the abolition of slavery.

Robert Owen founded the New Harmony community in 1825.

A New Capital City

Indianapolis was still a wilderness in 1820.

As more settlers poured into Indiana, they pushed farther north. Central Indiana had been granted to the Indians by treaty, but the federal government bought the area back in 1818 and opened it for settlement. This New Purchase region seemed to be a good site for a centrally located government, and Indianapolis became the new state capital in 1825. There was no statehouse at that point, so the government offices were set up in

The Indianapolis state capitol in the 1850s

the Marion County Courthouse. They moved into the brand-new capitol in 1835.

The new capital grew quickly, and its stores soon offered cloth, shoes, tools, clocks, stoves, and many other luxuries. But for ordinary farmers far from town, it was too hard to travel to big cities.

New Ways to Travel

In the 1820s, Indiana embarked on massive road- and canal-building projects. The National Road crossed central Indiana between Richmond and Terre Haute. For a north-south route, the Michigan

Road extended from northwest Indiana down to Madison. The Wabash and Erie Canal, which connected the Maumee and Wabash Rivers, extended into Ohio. It took twenty-five years and a whopping $25 million to construct. Unfortunately, all these building projects were so expensive that they plunged the state deeply into debt.

Indiana's first railroad was just a horse-drawn car that made its first run in 1834. In time, the tracks ran between Indianapolis and Madison. Madison, an Ohio River town in southeast Indiana, became the state's largest city in the 1840s. The railroad made it possible for merchants to send goods from Indianapolis to the Ohio and on down the Mississippi River. From the Mississippi port of New Orleans, the goods could be shipped to Europe.

The new railroads connected merchants to new far-flung markets.

William Henry Harrison was known as Old Tippecanoe.

William Henry Harrison had been the first governor of Indiana Territory, but he was best remembered for his victory in the Battle of Tippecanoe. His nickname, in fact, was Old Tippecanoe. When he ran for president in 1840 with running mate John Tyler, their campaign slogan was "Tippecanoe and Tyler too." Harrison won that election, only to die of pneumonia one month after taking office.

New railroads built in the 1850s made a big difference for farmers. Now they had a fast way to send their products to markets in the eastern United States. New coal mines, rock quarries, and factories opened near rail lines so they could ship their goods off too.

Indiana was prospering more than ever. Well-to-do farmers were able to build brick houses or even stately mansions. Thriving towns grew up at the junctions of major roads and railroads. Their shops offered a wide variety of goods, including luxurious items imported from Europe. For ladies, there were silk and brocade fabrics, hoop skirts, and fabulous hats. Men shopped for fashionable waistcoats, ruffled shirts, and beaver hats.

Slavery and the Civil War

Meanwhile, the issue of slavery was bringing the nation to a boiling point. Several proslavery Southern states withdrew from the rest of the country and declared themselves the Confederate States of America. In 1861, Confederates fired on Union troops at Fort Sumter in South Carolina, starting the Civil War. Although many of its residents had come from the South, Indiana supported the Union side and sent about 200,000 men off to battle.

The war never reached into Indiana except for one bizarre incident. In 1863, Confederate general John Hunt Morgan led his cavalrymen—Morgan's Raiders—from Kentucky into Indiana. They weren't really on a military mission. The Raiders stormed into

When Morgan's Raiders came through Indiana in 1863, they robbed farmhouses throughout the countryside.

A Stop on the Railroad

Here is an excerpt from Levi Coffin's memoirs about the Underground Railroad:

"We knew not what night or hour of the night we would be aroused by a gentle rap at the door. . . . I have often been awakened by this signal, and sprang out of bed and opened the door. Outside in the cold or the rain, there would be a two-horse wagon loaded with fugitives, perhaps the greater part of them women and children. I would invite them in a low tone to come in, and they would follow me into the darkened house without a word, for we knew not who might be watching or listening. When they were all safely inside and the door fastened, I would cover the windows, strike a light and build a good fire. By this time my wife would be up and preparing victuals for them, and in a short time the cold and hungry fugitives would be made comfortable. . . . The fugitives would rest on pallets before the fire the rest of the night." ■

Corydon, then tore through the countryside, robbing farmhouses and looting stores. They took food, water, horses, cash, and anything they could carry off—even clocks, birdcages, and bolts of cloth—before heading on into Ohio.

The Underground Railroad

Many people in Indiana supported slaves who were trying to escape from the South to freedom in Canada. Some Indiana residents joined a secret network called the Underground Railroad and helped smuggle escaping slaves to safety. This was a risky business, because it was against the law. Indiana's 1851 constitution barred blacks from entering the state, and the national Fugitive Slave Act made it a crime to harbor an escaped slave. Nevertheless, the movement went on, cloaked in the dark of night.

Many of the railroad's "operators" were members of the Quaker religion, a group firmly opposed to slavery. Fountain City, a Quaker community in eastern Indiana, came to be known as the Grand Central Station of the Underground Railroad.

Levi Coffin was a prominent resident of Fountain City. He and his wife, Katie, were deeply involved in helping fugitive slaves. It's estimated that they sheltered as many as 2,000 slaves on their way to Canada. In the Coffins' home, they could rest safely, eat heartily, and prepare for the journey ahead. According to tradition, one of the Coffins' fugitive guests was little Eliza, the heroine of Harriet Beecher Stowe's novel *Uncle Tom's Cabin.*

Levi Coffin helped escaping slaves on the Underground Railroad.

Fortunes Rise and Fall

The war created a high demand for Indiana's farm and factory goods. The state supplied machinery, cloth, and processed foods to the Union army.

After the Civil War ended in 1865, farmers were able to increase their production with mechanized plows and tractors. This worked well at first, but there was a downside. With more and more crops on the market, prices dropped. Many farmers had bor-

Benjamin Harrison

Benjamin Harrison (1833–1901) served as the twenty-third president from 1889 to 1893. Born in Ohio, he was the grandson of President William Henry Harrison. He became a successful lawyer in Indianapolis and fought in the Civil War. As a U.S. senator from Indiana, Harrison favored civil service reform, civil rights, and high import taxes to protect U.S. industry. He continued these efforts as president and pushed through many important laws in these areas. ■

rowed heavily to buy the new machines, figuring they could easily repay the debts after their rich harvests. Instead, the farmers were worse off than before. Meanwhile, Indiana's mining and manufacturing industries continued to expand.

Native Sons

For five elections in a row, Indianans had a native son running for either president or vice president. Governor Thomas A. Hendricks ran for vice president with Democratic candidate Samuel Tilden in 1876, but they lost. Democrat William H. English ran unsuccessfully for vice president in 1880. Hendricks tried for the vice presidency again in 1884 with presidential candidate Grover Cleveland. This time, he won.

Benjamin Harrison, grandson of William Henry Harrison, beat Grover Cleveland to win the presidency in 1888. Then Cleveland won the office back from Harrison in the election of 1892. The grandson of "Old Tippecanoe" returned to Indianapolis, where he was a respected lawyer, and enjoyed his children and grandchildren throughout his later years.

Thomas Hendricks served as vice president under Grover Cleveland.

CHAPTER FOUR

Into the Modern Age

Indiana continued its rapid industrial growth in the late 1800s. The fastest-growing area was the Calumet region—the strip of Lake Michigan shoreline where the cities of Hammond, Whiting, East Chicago, and Gary stand today. In just a few years, this stretch of swamps and sand dunes grew into one of the most industrialized regions in the United States.

The Rise of the Calumet Region

It all began when the Standard Oil Company laid pipelines from Ohio to the little village of Whiting. There, in 1889, the company built one of the largest oil refineries in the world. Its lakeshore location was perfect for shipping out tons of products. Other companies soon realized what a great site the Calumet region was. Many heavy industries opened in Hammond and East Chicago, and their port grew into one of the nation's greatest shipping centers.

Steel became the state's fastest-growing and most important industry. First, Inland Steel opened a plant in East Chicago in 1893. Then in 1906, the United States Steel Corporation began to erect massive steel mills along miles of Lake Michigan shoreline. This gave birth to the city of Gary. Thousands of workers including immigrants from Hungary, Italy, Poland, and other European countries, moved there to work in the mills. Like a magnet, Gary quickly attracted more businesses. They included not only steel companies such as Republic Steel and Inland Steel, but also DuPont, Sinclair, Shell, and other petroleum companies.

Cars—The Wave of the Future

Meanwhile, another industry appeared on the scene—newfangled horseless carriages called automobiles. In Kokomo, Elwood Haynes developed the first gasoline-powered, clutch-driven automobile with an electric ignition. On a sunny summer day in 1894, he took it to a back road outside of town for a test drive. He drove the machine for 1.5 miles (2.4 kilometers), reaching the amazing speed of 8 miles (13 km) per hour.

Haynes's success was quite interesting to Clement Studebaker and his brothers. Their wagon and carriage company in South Bend was the largest in the world. Clement knew that automobiles were the wave of the future and would be the next generation in transportation.

In 1897, the Studebakers began experimenting with electric-powered carriages. In 1902, the first Studebaker automobile made a successful run, and manufacturing began at once. Unfortunately, Clement did not live to see his vision come true; he died in 1901.

Elwood Haynes in 1894

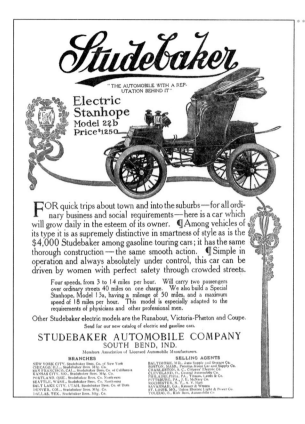

A 1907 Studebaker advertisement

But his brothers—John, Peter, and Jacob—carried on the business, making and selling Studebaker passenger cars and trucks.

When the United States entered World War I in 1917, Indiana contributed both fighting men and materials. Industrial plants supplied vehicles and other equipment, and farmers sent food. Women and children helped by assembling "comfort kits" for the soldiers. These were packs of homemade sweaters, socks, bandages, pajamas, and other essential supplies.

After the war, the high demand for farm products dropped—and so did the prices. Many Indiana farmers went out of business in the 1920s and moved on to work in factories and mills. For the first time in its history, Indiana had more residents in cities than in rural areas.

Depression and War

Even more farms failed after 1929, when the United States plunged into the Great Depression. Banks and businesses across the nation collapsed, and Indiana suffered badly too. In both large cities and small towns, thousands of people lost their jobs. In southern Indiana, coal mines and stone quarries closed down, leaving much of the population out of work.

To relieve the situation, the state and federal governments set up a number of social aid programs. Unemployment compensation,

The depression brought poverty to many Indiana families.

public welfare, social security, and many other such programs began during this difficult time. Southern Indiana took another hit when the Ohio River flooded in 1937. Entire cities were underwater, hundreds of people drowned, and thousands were left homeless.

In spite of the depression, many of Indiana's heavy industries survived. When the United States entered World War II in 1941, Indiana's factory goods were in high demand. By the end of the war in 1945, the state was truly back on its feet.

Economic Ups and Downs

A factory production line during World War II

In the 1950s, Indiana invested in massive road building, with new paved highways crisscrossing the state. The Indiana Toll Road opened in 1956, and wide interstate highways made it fast and easy to drive to neighboring states.

More and more factories switched to automated production in the 1960s. New machinery, electronic assembly lines, and computerized design were exciting developments in manufacturing. But the downside was that the new methods eliminated many jobs. In

some cities, unemployment soared. South Bend was hit harder than most cities when its Studebaker plant closed down in 1963.

Studebaker workers in 1941, when the company was thriving

The Port of Indiana, which opened in 1970, was a great boost for the state's economy. This deepwater port at Burns Harbor on Lake Michigan could service oceangoing vessels that entered the St. Lawrence Seaway from the Atlantic Ocean. Thanks to Burns Harbor, Indiana industries could ship more products in and out directly. They were able to skip the "middlemen"—all the intermediate freight carriers they needed before.

Tough Competition

Competition with foreign goods is a problem for industries all over the United States. Cheaply made products from overseas arrive on the market here, and they sell for such low prices that American-made goods often have trouble competing.

This has a good side and a bad side. On the one hand, it keeps U.S. manufacturers "on their toes" by inspiring them to find more efficient ways to make things. On the other hand, it can force U.S. firms to shut down if they can't drop their prices low enough or fast enough to keep up with the competition.

In the 1980s, imported steel severely hurt the nation's steel industry. As a top steel producer, Indiana was hit hard. Many steel mills had to cut production or close down altogether, leaving thousands of people out of work. As people left the state to find jobs, the population growth slowed down. Fewer tax-paying residents, in turn, meant that the state had less money to spend on improvements and social services.

Indiana's economy bounced back in the 1990s. One reason for that growth spurt is the state's development of high-technology and service industries. These industries keep the economy from depending so heavily on manufacturing.

Indiana Today and Tomorrow

Today, Indiana suffers from many of the problems that plague the rest of the country. But the state government has been aggressive in attacking its problems. By raising taxes, the state has more money to put into programs that attract new business. Deteriorating city centers are a nationwide concern, and many Indiana cities are refurbishing their downtown areas so that people can enjoy them more. Indianapolis now glistens with new office buildings and sports centers.

State leaders are also investing more tax dollars in education. The extra effort is paying off. National test scores in many of Indiana's school districts are rising. And in the late 1990s, Indiana's school science programs were ranked first in the nation. This is great news for Hoosiers, because their young people are the key to a bright future in the twenty-first century!

Downtown Indianapolis is an example of the state's many refurbished urban areas.

CHAPTER FIVE

Over the Hills and Plains

Some people describe Indiana's landscape in just one word—*flat*. But when they take a closer look, they realize that there's much more going on! It's true that monstrous glaciers crunched across the terrain tens of thousands of years ago and ground the surface down. But as the glaciers advanced and retreated, they created dips, swells, ridges, knobs—and an intriguing network of underground caverns.

The Till Plains

The fertile, rolling plains that cover central Indiana are called the Tipton Till. During the Ice Age, great glaciers—slowly moving sheets of ice—slid across the land. As they advanced, the glaciers deposited sediment called till, consisting of sand, silt, clay, and huge stones. As the glaciers melted, they left sand and gravel behind.

Opposite: A cornfield outside Greenwood

The rich Indiana soil is good for growing wheat as well as other crops.

Putting Indiana in Its Place

In size, Indiana ranks thirty-eighth among the fifty states. Indiana's northwest corner touches Lake Michigan, while the state of Michigan forms the rest of the northern border. Illinois lies to the west of Indiana, and Ohio is on the east. The Ohio River runs along Indiana's southern border, and across the river is Kentucky. ▪

All these materials settled in Indiana's valleys, creating the gently rolling landscape we see today. Central Indiana is part of the corn belt that stretches across the nation's Midwest. Its rich soil is ideal for growing corn and other grains and for grazing cattle.

Strangely enough, Indiana's highest point is in the Till Plains. A hilltop in far-eastern Wayne County rises 1,257 feet (383 meters) above sea level.

The Great Lakes Plains

Northern Indiana falls within the Great Lakes Plains. This region, too, was flattened by glaciers, but some areas are quite high and hilly. The Northern Lake and Moraine Region of northeastern Indiana is noted for its beautiful scenery. Moraines are high ridges formed by melting glaciers.

Huge sand dunes rise along the shore of Lake Michigan. The lake deposited sand on the beach thousands of years ago as its water level slowly sank. Winds blowing in from the lake formed great sand dunes.

The dunes closest to the lake are the youngest, while the dunes farther inland are the oldest. Some are still quite sandy, while others are covered with grasses and other vegetation. Much of the remaining dune area is protected as Indiana Dunes National Lakeshore.

Lake Michigan along the Indiana Dunes National Lakeshore

The Smoking Dune

Mount Baldy, at 123 feet (38 m), is one of the largest dunes on Lake Michigan's shore. It's known as a "live dune" because it's still being blown along by the wind.

Baldy moves 4 to 5 feet (1.2 to 1.5 m) farther from the lake every year. It's often called the "smoking dune" because the sand blowing off the top looks like wisps of smoke. ■

The Southern Hills and Lowlands

Glaciers never reached south-central Indiana. The hills and lowlands here follow the rises and dips in the bedrock beneath the surface soil. In some places, the bedrock crops out in the form of knobs, or steep hills. The biggest "dip" slopes toward the southwest, and Indiana's southwestern tip is the state's lowest point. At

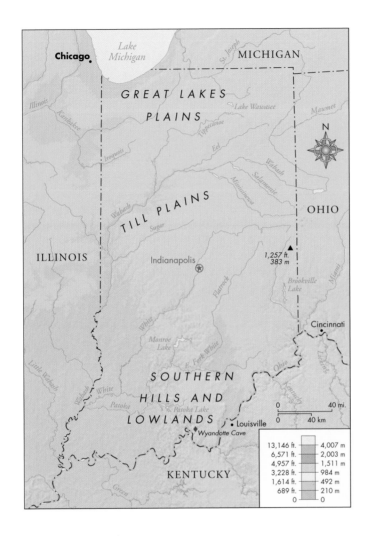

Indiana's topography

the meeting point of the Wabash and Ohio Rivers, it is just 320 feet (98 m) above sea level. This region is also rich in coal and petroleum.

Much of the state's bedrock is limestone, and south-central Indiana is sometimes called limestone country. Bedford blossomed as a limestone-quarrying town more than a century ago.

Sunrise on the Ohio River

Caves and caverns are common in this region too. Over time, the natural acids in rain and snow dissolved the limestone, creating hollowed-out caves and underground streams. Bluespring Cavern near Bedford is one of the ten largest caves in the world. Other spectacular underground wonders are Wyandotte and Marengo Caves in the far south.

Wyandotte Cave

Wyandotte Cave, near Leavenworth, is one of the largest caverns in the United States. One of its huge chambers is called Rothrock Cathedral. Rising inside the chamber is a limestone "mountain" 135 feet (41 m) high. Visitors can take tours that last from half an hour to a whole day. On some of these tours, people hike along steep underground trails and squeeze their bodies through extremely narrow and low passageways. ■

Rivers and Lakes

The Ohio River, which forms Indiana's entire southern border, is the main eastern branch of the mighty Mississippi. The Wabash River, a tributary of the Ohio, flows from Ohio all the way across Indiana. The Wabash outlines part of Indiana's western border before emptying into the Ohio River.

Rafting along the Mississinewa River

Another of Indiana's major rivers is the White River. It flows southwestward across central Indiana, joining the Wabash in the southwest corner of the state. The Tippecanoe River is also a tributary of the Wabash. So are the Eel, Mississinewa, and Salamonie Rivers. In the east, the St. Marys and St. Joseph Rivers join at Fort Wayne to form the Maumee River, which empties into Lake Erie at Toledo, Ohio.

Indiana's Geographical Features

Total area; rank	36,420 sq. mi. (94,328 sq km); 38th
Land area; rank	35,870 sq. mi. (92,903 sq km); 38th
Water area; rank	550 sq. mi. (1,425 sq km); 38th
Inland water; **rank**	315 sq. mi. (816 sq km); 42nd
Great Lakes water; **rank**	235 sq. mi. (608 sq km); 8th
Geographic center	Boone, 14 miles (23 km) northwest of Indianapolis
Highest point	In Wayne County, 1,257 feet (383 m) above sea level
Lowest point	In Posey County, 320 feet (98 m) above sea level
Largest city	Indianapolis
Population; rank	5,564,228 (1990 census); 14th
Record high temperature	116°F (47°C) at Collegeville on July 14, 1936
Record low temperature	−35°F (−37°C) at Greensburg on February 2, 1951
Average July temperature	75°F (24°C)
Average January temperature	28°F (−2°C)
Average annual precipitation	40 inches (102 cm)

Monroe Lake, near Bloomington, is Indiana's largest artificial lake. Many of the state's natural lakes are in the Northern Lake and Moraine Region. Lake Wawasee is the largest natural lake in the state. Others include Manitou, Maxinkuckee, and Turkey Lakes. Lake Michigan, of course, is larger than them all. Along with the other Great Lakes, it was formed when the Ice Age glaciers melted.

Some of Indiana's lakes are called kettle lakes. They're shaped like a kettle filled with water. Kettle lakes were created during the time of the glaciers. Sometimes, a glacier left behind an enormous block of ice. As the glacier moved along, the ice block became buried in the sediment. Over time, the ice melted, leaving a kettle-shaped hole filled with water.

Grasses, Trees, and Strange Plants

When European settlers first arrived, prairie grasses waved over about one-fifth of what is now Indiana. Dense forests covered the rest of the land—as many as 20 million acres (8 million hectares). Today, about one-sixth of the state is forestland. In many areas, new trees have been planted to replace those that were cleared for farming and lumbering. But fewer than 2,000 acres (810 ha) of Indiana's old-growth forests remain.

Sycamores, oaks, maples, and beeches are Indiana's most common hardwood trees. Ashes, willows, elms, and tulip trees (the state tree) are abundant too. Walnut and hickory trees bear delicious nuts and provide wood for commercial lumber.

Many strange and surprising plants grow in Indiana. Prickly pear cactuses and orchids are found in moist, sandy areas. Carnivorous, or flesh-eating, plants

Maples are among the trees that grow in Indiana.

grow in the northeastern lake region. They include pitcher plants, sundews, and bladderworts. These plants don't eat humans or animals, though—just insects!

Creatures in the Wild

Take a walk through Indiana's woodlands and prairies, and listen to the rustling sounds of animals scurrying about. Rabbits, raccoons, squirrels, opossums, foxes, skunks, muskrats, woodchucks, weasels, moles, and mice are among Indiana's native wild animals. Most of the large animals that once roamed the forests are gone—except for deer. They are so plentiful that people are now allowed to hunt them at certain times of the year.

Black bears, elks, lynxes, mountain lions, porcupines, and wolverines used to live in Indiana too. But they have gradually disappeared over the years as people hunted them and cleared their habitats for farmland. Some of the animals that still live in Indiana are in danger of becoming extinct, such as badgers, bobcats, river otters, gray and red wolves, and several types of bat.

Some of the birds that flit through Indiana's meadows and woods are blue jays, sparrows, wrens, swallows, warblers, orioles, wood thrushes, and cardinals—the state bird. Game birds such as quails, wild turkeys, and pheasants strut around the forest floor searching for insects and seeds. Among the predator birds are hawks and owls. Wetlands and shores are alive with ducks, geese, egrets, herons, and other waterbirds. Indiana's endangered bird species include bald eagles, peregrine falcons, piping plovers, trumpeter swans, and yellow-headed blackbirds.

Insect-eating pitcher plants

Indiana's parks and forests

When it's time to go fishing, most people are hoping to catch salmon or trout. Indiana's lakes and streams also abound with pike, bass, catfish, pickerel, and sunfish.

Indiana's Seasons

Hoosiers have learned to expect snow within the six-month span from November through April. An average of about 20 inches

Are You My Mother?

Trumpeter swans are learning to migrate from Ontario, Canada, to southern Indiana by following an airplane. In December 1998, four young swans followed an ultralight aircraft 675 miles (1,086 km) to Muscatatuck National Wildlife Refuge in southern Indiana. The lakes, ponds, and wetlands there make it a perfect wintering place.

Scientists hope this trip will establish a new migration route for the swans. It's part of a project to build up a migrating flock in eastern North America. Researchers believe that swans find their migratory destinations by geographic features they see from the air. Young swans ordinarily follow their parents on a migration, but the swans in this experiment are trained to follow the plane.

Trumpeter swans are named for their deep, resonating calls. They are huge—the largest waterfowl in North America and the largest swans in the world. An adult is about 4 feet (1.2 m) long with an 8-foot (2.4-m) wingspan. They have long necks and are entirely white, with jet-black bills and feet. ■

(51 centimeters) of snow falls on Indiana in a year. But the far north can get as much as 100 inches (254 cm) a year.

In northwest Indiana, the "lake effect" creates more snow, but keeps temperatures milder. Lake Michigan warms the air so that it readily condenses into moisture such as rain and snow. But that same warm air also acts as a buffer, protecting the lakeshore from bitterly cold air currents.

Spring is tornado season across the Midwest, and Indiana has its share of twisters. In addition, spring rains make the Ohio River swell, and springtime flooding can be a hazard in river valley towns. While northern Indiana gets more snow, the southern part of the state gets more rain. Late summer droughts sometimes

A winter sunset in Turkey Run State Park

plague southern Indiana, where August and September are the driest months of the year. Still, farmers in southern Indiana enjoy a longer growing season overall than farmers in the northern part of the state.

Many tourists choose fall as their favorite time to visit Indiana. The people who live there also find the autumn a great time to be outdoors. All over the state, woodlands and forests are ablaze with the spectacular colors of changing leaves—the brilliant oranges, dazzling yellows, and deep-scarlet reds of maples, oaks, yellow poplars, and many more. Walking through the woods is a delight for the senses as people see the colors, smell the woodsy aroma, and hear the rustle of leaves underfoot.

Autumn at Weston Lake

CHAPTER SIX

Exploring Indiana

The Michigan City Lighthouse

A tour of Indiana reveals a variety of "layers." There are magnificent natural areas that existed long before humans ever came on the scene. Then there is the historic layer—Native American sites, pioneer settlements, battlefields, and forts. Finally, scattered amidst nature and history, are Indiana's bustling centers of business and culture.

Northern Indiana

Northern Indiana is the state's most industrial region. Along the northwest corridor, the night sky glows from the furnaces of steel mills. Gary and Hammond are the major cities in the northwest Calumet region. Though they have been hurt by pollution and unemployment, they take pride in refurbishing their neighborhoods and city centers. One example is Gary's Genesis Convention Center, a sparkling white venue for concerts and sports events.

Opposite: A summer dawn at Chain O' Lakes State Park

Just to the east is some of the state's most beautiful scenery, with sand dunes rolling gently along the horizon. Indiana Dunes National Lakeshore offers miles of spectacular beaches, as well as lakes and wooded parks. In Michigan City is the three-story Barker Mansion, once the home of an area industrialist. Its floors and walls are made of marble and rare woods, and the original furniture and artworks remain.

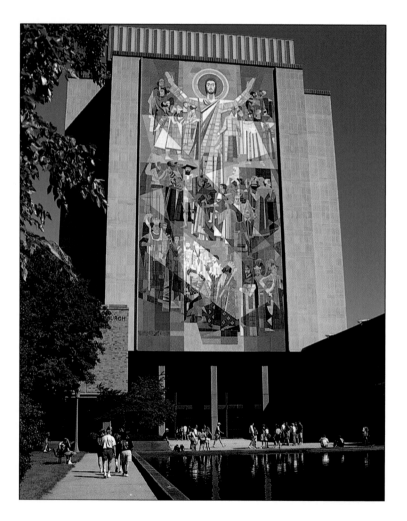

"Touchdown Jesus" at Notre Dame

South Bend's most famous site is the University of Notre Dame. Its Golden Dome glitters atop the administration building. For football fans, a more famous landmark on campus is "Touchdown Jesus." This gigantic mosaic, with upraised arms, adorns the face of the Theodore M. Hesburgh Library—looming (so it seems) over the Fighting Irish football field.

Studebakers were popular family cars in the 1940s and 1950s, but they were no longer produced after their South Bend manufacturing plant closed in 1963. Now the city's Studebaker National Museum honors not only "Studes" but also more than a century of other vehicles—from Conestoga wagons to modern Avantis.

Many Amish communities dot the countryside in Elkhart and Lagrange Counties. Amish farmers are often seen tilling their fields with horse-drawn plows and driving along country roads in horse-drawn buggies. Family-owned Amish stores sell delicious homemade apple butter, as well as handmade furniture, quilts, and other craft items.

Amish Acres in Nappanee is a restored farm where visitors can tour the house and barn, watch craft demonstrations, and take a buggy ride. The Menno-Hof Mennonite-Amish Visitors Center in Shipshewana offers a glimpse of the history, beliefs, and lifestyle of these simple, devout people.

Elkhart County is home to a number of Amish communities.

Indiana's cities and interstates

Have you ever heard someone say "that's a real doozie" when they meant something was really special? The word is really "Duesey"—short for Duesenberg. This sleek, high-class car of the 1920s was handcrafted in Auburn. Now the Auburn-Cord-Duesenberg Museum displays many of these classic cars. Every September, Auburn is the site of America's largest classic car auction.

Fort Wayne started out in 1680 as a French outpost called Fort Miami. The British seized it in 1760, and General "Mad Anthony" Wayne later rebuilt it. Today, people wearing uniforms of the period reenact military maneuvers in the reconstructed fort. Fort Wayne's Lincoln Museum holds the world's largest private collection of Abraham Lincoln memorabilia.

The Fort Wayne skyline

Central Indiana

The rolling plains of central Indiana have the best farmland in the state. Pioneers discovered this long ago, and many reminders of their lifestyle remain in the region today.

Parke County, in the far west, has thirty-two covered bridges from the nineteenth century—more than any other county in the United States. Three of them are in Rockville's Billie Creek Village. Visitors to this pioneer settlement can enjoy a horse-drawn wagon ride and tour thirty historic buildings.

In nearby Terre Haute, Fowler Park Pioneer Village offers another glimpse of pioneer life in its many log buildings. The Vigo County Historical Museum showcases the region's rich history. One famous item on display there is an original Coca-Cola bottle. It was designed by the Root Glass Company, once a booming industry in the town. Terre Haute's Inland Aquatics contains the largest coral reef display in the United States.

Crawfordsville's most famous resident was Lew Wallace, author of the epic novel *Ben-Hur.* The town has a wonderful array of buildings in classic architectural style.

In the fall, Big Ten football fans flock to Purdue University's Ross Ade Stadium in West Lafayette. At halftime, the marching band rolls out its giant drum—8 feet (2.4 m) high and 4 feet (1.2 m) wide.

Just outside of Lafayette is Tippecanoe Battlefield, where William Henry Harrison

William Henry Harrison's statue is part of the Tippecanoe Battlefield Monument.

battled the Shawnee Prophet. At Imagination Station in Lafayette, kids can do hands-on science experiments.

Years before Henry Ford built the Model T, Elwood Haynes came up with an automobile of his own. A Kokomo museum named after Haynes displays his car and his many other inventions. Mississinewa Battlefield in Marion is the site of America's first victory in the War of 1812.

It's always 1836 at Conner Prairie in Noblesville. Visitors can join the costumed "settlers" as they go about their chores and games in this restored pioneer village. Among its thirty buildings

Conner Prairie is a restored pioneer village.

are the mansion of pioneer William Conner and a log cabin that was once the town trading post.

"Hoosier Hysteria" reigns supreme in New Castle. It's the home of the world's largest high school field house, as well as the Indiana Basketball Hall of Fame Museum.

The Whitewater Canal closed down in 1860, but a 15-mile (24-km) stretch is preserved in Metamora as Whitewater Canal State Historic Site. Aboard the horse-drawn canal boat *Ben Franklin*, visitors can experience travel as in days gone by. There's an old gristmill for grinding corn into cornmeal, and the town's original wooden buildings are now shops.

When Quakers first moved into Indiana, they settled in Richmond. One famous member of their community was Levi Coffin, who lived in nearby Fountain City. His home, now a museum, was a famous stop on the Underground Railroad. Coffin and his wife helped as many as 2,000 slaves escape to freedom.

Indianapolis

Indiana's capital city is a modern, gleaming metropolis rising above the plains. The city planners designed it with two of the world's great cities in mind—Washington, D.C., and Versailles, France. Indianapolis is a major midwestern transportation hub, where many highways and railroads meet.

As modern as it is, Indianapolis still honors its history. The Soldiers and Sailors Monument, right in the center of town, is a shrine to all those citizens who died defending their country.

The brand-new Indiana Historical Society building houses many treasures of the state's history, both old and new. Besides its

**The Soldiers and
Sailors Monument in
downtown Indianapolis**

An exhibit in the Eiteljorg Museum of American Indians and Western Art

rare old books and photos, it features a Sounds of Indiana room. Music lovers of all kinds can revel in the strains of Indiana musicians Cole Porter, John Mellencamp, and many others.

State leaders carry on their business in the Indiana state capitol, with its copper dome soaring over the marble-columned rotunda. Nearby in Circle Centre stands the ultramodern Artsgarden, a glass-and-steel landmark rising seven stories above street level. Hilbert Circle Theatre is the home of the Indianapolis Symphony Orchestra. The Indianapolis Museum of Art and the Eiteljorg Museum of American Indians and Western Art are two of the city's fine museums.

On Memorial Day weekend in May, the Indianapolis Motor Speedway hosts the rip-roaring Indianapolis 500 auto race. More people attend this race than any other one-day event in the world. The speedway's Hall of Fame museum is open all year.

Rolling Hills and River Towns

Southern Indiana's landscape makes a striking contrast to the cornfields and plains farther north. Here there are dense forests, lush valleys, steep bluffs, deep gorges, and a maze of limestone caverns. The region is steeped in history too. With the Ohio River coursing along its border, southern Indiana was the first part of the state that pioneers settled.

Historically, Vincennes is one of Indiana's most significant cities. The George Rogers Clark National Historical Park commemorates the Revolutionary War hero's capture of Fort Sackville there in 1779. Clark's victory marked the largest land conquest of the American Revolution.

Vincennes was also the capital of Indiana Territory. Its downtown historic district includes the old capitol, as well as a print shop and state bank from that period. President William Henry Harrison lived in Vincennes. His house, called Grouseland, is open to visitors. The Indiana Military Museum, also located in Vincennes, has collections that cover U.S. military history from the Civil War to the Persian Gulf War.

George Rogers Clark National Historical Park

Most of Indiana's Amish people live in the northeast, but many Amish communities also thrive in Daviess County, east of Vincennes. Their neatly kept farms cover the rolling hills, and their shops are chock-full of delicious bakery goods, handmade quilts, and other traditional craft items.

Bloomington, the home of Indiana University, is also the site of the fascinating Lilly Library. Building on the collection of pharmaceutical magnate J. K. Lilly, the library holds thousands of rare books, including a Gutenberg Bible.

Traveling through Brown County, just east of Bloomington, is like taking a step back in time. Old log cabins still stand on many of the farms that cover the rolling hillsides.

Many artists were enthralled with the beauty of this region and settled there to paint the wooded scenery. The most famous was

The clock tower at Indiana University

Theodore Clement (T. C.) Steele, who arrived in 1907. His home in Nashville is now a historic site. Visitors can stroll through his eleven-room home, studio, cabin, and wildflower gardens and view his impressionist paintings. In town, craft shops exhibit weavings, fine woodworkings, pottery, and many other crafts.

Nearby Brown County State Park is the largest in the state. Miles of hiking and horseback-riding trails meander through its forested hills and alongside winding creeks.

The town of Columbus is renowned as a showplace of beautiful architecture. More than fifty of its public buildings were designed by famous architects.

Antiques, boutiques, and little cafés await visitors to Madison, a historic town on the banks of the Ohio River. Because of its interesting architecture, an amazing 133 square blocks of Madison are listed on the National Register of Historic Places. The Ohio River National Scenic Byway passes Madison and meanders along the river. It offers spectacular views of the countryside, the river, and the many quaint river towns.

Not far downriver from Madison is Falls of the Ohio State Park. It is not only a beautiful recreation area, it is also a famous prehistoric site. Lying in plain sight are fossil beds that are 400 million years old. The fossils were formed when aquatic animals sank to the bottom of the river and became

Madison is known for its historic homes.

exposed as the water level dropped. In the nearby town of Starlight, visitors to the Forest Discovery Center can stroll through a lifelike model forest and visit a model logging plant.

Hoosier National Forest covers a vast section of south-central Indiana. In the center is Patoka Lake, a huge reservoir surrounded by wildlife and recreation areas. To the north, in West Baden

A view of Hoosier National Forest

Springs, is the West Baden Springs Hotel. An architectural wonder built in 1902, it has been restored to its days of grandeur. Visitors feel dwarfed when they enter the atrium, with its dome six stories overhead and giant-sized stone urns.

Near the southern reaches of Hoosier National Forest, tucked out of sight beneath the earth, are the winding passageways of many caves and caverns. Marengo Cave has a magnificent underground room called the Crystal Palace. Deep inside Wyandotte Cave in Leavenworth rises the highest underground mountain in the world. The cave also contains the world's largest stalagmite pillar.

Corydon was Indiana's first capital. Now the restored limestone capitol, the governor's residence, and the old town square are preserved as state historic sites. Daniel Boone and his brother Squire Boone discovered a cave near Corydon in 1790. While Daniel pushed westward, Squire settled in the area. His dying wish was to be buried in the cave, and there he now rests.

Abraham Lincoln and his family moved to southern Indiana in 1816, and it was there he grew into a young man. The Lincoln Boyhood National Memorial near Lincoln City re-creates a typical farm of his time and preserves the gravesite of Lincoln's mother. Nearby Lincoln State Park presents the musical drama *Young Abe Lincoln* in the summertime.

Residents of Evansville enjoy the peaceful river scenery as they stroll alongside the meandering Ohio. Riverside Drive is the scene of the city's summertime Riverfest, with food, music, rides, a 5-K marathon, and a talent show. People can even enjoy the scenery when they're at Evansville's zoo. A tram takes visitors over the rolling hills of Mesker Park Zoo and Botanic Garden. The zoo

A popular tourist destination in southern Indiana is Abraham Lincoln's restored boyhood home in Lincoln City.

houses more than 700 animals and features a butterfly exhibit during the summer.

One of the most important prehistoric sites in the country lies just outside of Evansville. It is called Angel Mounds—named after the farmer who once owned the land. Mississippian Indians lived there from 1100 to 1450, and eleven of their earthen platform mounds can still be seen.

In the southwest corner of the state, historic New Harmony preserves the settlements of the Harmonists and Owenites. These two communities tried to build societies where everyone worked for the common good. Though their beliefs were based on admirable principles, both communities eventually died out. What did *not* die is the typical Hoosier spirit—the imagination to experiment with new ideas and the courage to try them out!

Historic New Harmony as it looks today

CHAPTER SEVEN

Governing the Hoosier State

ndiana adopted its first constitution when it became a state in 1816. That constitution remained in effect until a new one was approved in 1851. The 1851 constitution is still in force today, although many amendments, or changes, have been added.

When citizens want to add a new amendment to the constitution, they must convince one of their representatives in the general assembly to propose it. Then both houses of the legislature must approve the amendment—twice. First, the current members of the legislature vote on the amendment. Then, after another election, the new legislature must approve it too.

Indiana's state government is organized just like the national government in Washington, D.C. Ruling power is divided among three branches of government—the executive, legislative, and judicial branches. This system makes sure there is always a balance of power, so that no one group becomes too strong.

Opposite: The capitol
and its surrounding
area

The State Flag and Seal

Indiana's state flag features a flaming golden torch and golden stars against a field of blue. The torch stands for liberty and en-lightenment, and their far-reaching effects are shown in the golden rays streaming out from the torch. The outer circle of thirteen stars stands for the thirteen original states. The five stars on the inner arc represent the next five states to enter the Union. Indiana, the nineteenth state, is the large star directly above the flame, with the word "Indiana" in a half-circle above it. The general assembly adopted this design in 1917 as part of Indiana's 1916 centennial celebration.

The state seal shows three hills in the center, with one tree on the left and two sycamore trees on the right. The sun is setting behind the hills, with fourteen rays coming out—thirteen rays for the original colonies and the fourteenth representing Indiana. On the right is a woodsman with an axe, and there is a buffalo jumping over a log to his right. On the ground are shoots of blue grass. Above the center are the words "Seal of the State of Indiana," and underneath is "1816"—the year of Indiana's statehood. On both sides of the date are diamonds with dots and leaves of the tulip tree, the state tree. The state seal was adopted in 1963. ■

Indiana's State Symbols

State bird: Cardinal Cardinals (left), or redbirds, live in Indiana year-round. They have a crest on their heads and strong, thick beaks for breaking seeds open. The male is bright red, and the female is brown with a dull red crest, wings, and tail. Cardinals build their nests in bushes or on low tree branches. The female lays two to four bluish white eggs with brown speckles. In 1932, when Indiana's people were debating over the state bird, the rose-breasted grosbeak and the Baltimore oriole were also considered. But cardinals won out in 1933. The cardinal is also the state bird of Illinois, Ohio, Virginia, West Virginia, Kentucky, and North Carolina.

State tree: Tulip tree The tulip tree is also known as the yellow poplar, but it's really a member of the magnolia family. Found throughout the state, it has broad, roundish leaves and greenish yellow, bell-shaped flowers that bloom in May or June. Tulip trees grow tall and straight and have soft, white wood. They're the tallest broadleaf trees in North America's eastern forests, growing as high as 200 feet (61 m). Their scientific name is *Liriodendron tulipifera.* The blossom of the tulip tree was Indiana's state flower from 1923 to 1931. The same year the flower lost its status, the tulip tree became the state's official tree. Tulip tree leaves appear on Indiana's state seal.

State flower: Peony Peonies (top right) produce large, gorgeous blossoms in shades of red, pink, and white. They bloom in late May or early June. When peonies begin to grow buds, their sweet nectar often attracts ants. By separating the petals, the ants help the flowers to open. The peony is actually Indiana's fourth state flower. The state adopted the carnation in 1913, but some people complained that carnations were native to Europe. In 1923, the tulip tree blossom became the official flower, and the zinnia took over in 1931. In the 1950s, zinnia fans and tulip tree supporters began to quarrel. Finally, in 1957, a bill came up in the general assembly to return the tulip tree blossom to its place of honor. But senators surprised everyone by preferring the dogwood blossom, while a representative who grew peonies suggested his own favorite flower. He

won. On March 13, 1957, the peony became the official state flower.

State rock: Limestone Limestone is a type of rock formation found in central and southern Indiana. It is mined from quarries and used in constructing buildings throughout the state. Indiana also exports its limestone to other states and all over the world. The stone was used to build the Empire State Building in New York City and the Washington National Cathedral in Washington, D.C. Limestone was formed more than 250 million years ago. It's made of the fossilized shells of tiny marine animals that sank to the bottom of the sea that once covered Indiana. As more and more sediment covered them, the pressure compressed the shells into rock. Given more time and more pressure, the same material becomes marble.

State river: Wabash River The Wabash River (bottom right) rises in Ohio and flows west and south across the entire state of Indiana. In the southwest, it forms part of the Indiana-Illinois border, where it flows into the Ohio River. The Wabash played an important role in Indiana's settlement and is memorialized in the state song. Its name comes from a Native American word for limestone.

Indiana's State Song
"On the Banks of the Wabash, Far Away"

Words and music by Paul Dresse
The state legislature adopted this as the official song in 1913.

'Round my Indiana homestead wave the cornfields,
In the distance loom the woodlands clear and cool.
Oftentimes my thoughts revert to scenes of childhood,
Where I first received my lessons, nature's school.
But one thing there is missing in the picture,
Without her face it seems so incomplete,
I long to see my mother in the doorway,
As she stood there years ago, her boy to greet.

Chorus:
Oh, the moonlight's fair tonight along the Wabash,
From the fields there comes the breath of new-mown hay,
Through the sycamores the candle lights are gleaming,
On the banks of the Wabash, far away.

Many years have passed since I strolled by the river,
Arm in arm, with sweetheart Mary by my side,
It was there I tried to tell her that I loved her,
It was there I begged of her to be my bride.
Long years have passed since I strolled thro' the churchyard.
She's sleeping there, my angel, Mary dear,
I loved her, but she thought I didn't mean it,
Still I'd give my future were she only here.

(Chorus)

The Executive Branch

The duty of the executive branch is to see that state laws are carried out. The governor is Indiana's chief executive officer and the head of the executive branch of government.

The governor and lieutenant governor run for office as a pair. Every four years, voters elect them and six other officials in the executive branch: the secretary of state, auditor, treasurer, attorney general, superintendent of public schools, and clerk of the supreme and appellate courts. All these officers may serve for any number of terms, but only two terms in a row.

The governor appoints the heads of almost all the state's commissions, departments, and institutions. When the governor is working out the state budget, he or she also sets the salaries for all these officials. Not many states give their governor that much power over state officers.

The Legislative Branch

Indiana's general assembly is the state's legislature, or lawmaking body. Like the U.S. Congress, it is bicameral—made up of two houses—the senate and the house of representatives. The fifty state senators serve four-year terms, while the one hundred state representatives serve for two years at a time.

Voters elect the legislators from districts whose boundaries are drawn according to population. Each district has roughly the same number of residents. By law, the districts must be reapportioned, or redrawn, every ten years after the national census is taken. This allows for shifts in population and makes sure that all citizens are fairly represented.

Governor Frank O'Bannon in 1999

The 100 members of the house of representatives meet in these chambers.

Indiana's Governors

Name	Party	Term	Name	Party	Term
Jonathan Jennings	Dem.-Rep.	1816–1822	Winfield T. Durbin	Rep.	1901–1905
Ratliff Boon	Dem.-Rep.	1822	J. Frank Hanly	Rep.	1905–1909
William Hendricks	Dem.-Rep.	1822–1825	Thomas R. Marshall	Dem.	1909–1913
James B. Ray	Ind.	1825–1831	Samuel M. Ralston	Dem.	1913–1917
Noah Noble	Whig	1831–1837	James P. Goodrich	Rep.	1917–1921
David Wallace	Whig	1837–1840	Warren T. McCray	Rep.	1921–1924
Samuel Bigger	Whig	1840–1843	Emmett Forest Branch	Rep.	1924–1925
James Whitcomb	Dem.	1843–1848	Ed Jackson	Rep.	1925–1929
Paris C. Dunning	Dem.	1848–1849	Harry G. Leslie	Rep.	1929–1933
Joseph A. Wright	Dem.	1849–1857	Paul V. McNutt	Dem.	1933–1937
Ashbel P. Willard	Dem.	1857–1860	M. Clifford Townsend	Dem.	1937–1941
Abram A. Hammond	Dem.	1860–1861	Henry F. Schricker	Dem.	1941–1945
Henry Smith Lane	Rep.	1861	Ralph F. Gates	Rep.	1945–1949
Oliver P. Morton	Rep.	1861–1867	Henry F. Schricker	Dem.	1949–1953
Conrad Baker	Rep.	1867–1873	George N. Craig	Rep.	1953–1957
Thomas A. Hendricks	Dem.	1873–1877	Harold W. Handley	Rep.	1957–1961
James D. Williams	Dem.	1877–1880	Matthew E. Welsh	Dem.	1961–1965
Isaac P. Gray	Dem.	1880–1881	Roger D. Branigin	Dem.	1965–1969
Albert G. Porter	Rep.	1881–1885	Edgar D. Whitcomb	Rep.	1969–1973
Isaac P. Gray	Dem.	1885–1889	Otis R. Bowen	Rep.	1973–1981
Alvin P. Hovey	Rep.	1889–1891	Robert D. Orr	Rep.	1981–1989
Ira Joy Chase	Rep.	1891–1893	Evan Bayh	Dem.	1989–1997
Claude Matthews	Dem.	1893–1897	Frank L. O'Bannon	Dem.	1997–
James A. Mount	Rep.	1897–1901			

The general assembly holds regular sessions every year, beginning by the second Monday in January. Sessions in odd-numbered years last sixty-one business days. They may not run any later than April 29. Sessions in even-numbered years meet for thirty days and cannot last past March 14. If there is urgent business to discuss at other times, the governor may call a special session that can last up to thirty days.

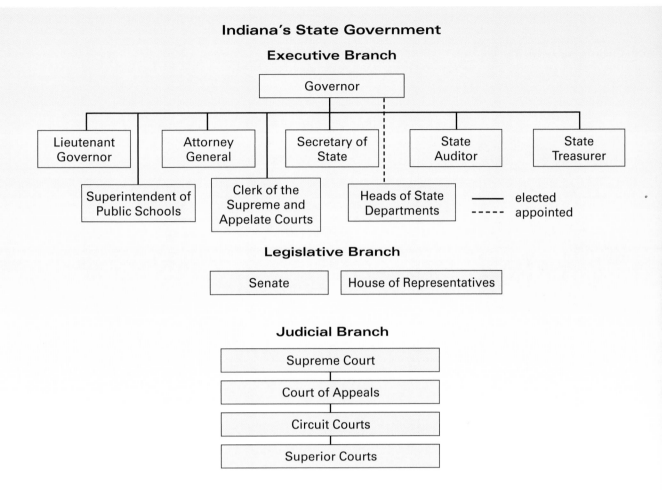

Indiana's State Government

Executive Branch

- Governor
  - Lieutenant Governor
    - Superintendent of Public Schools
  - Attorney General
  - Clerk of the Supreme and Appelate Courts
  - Secretary of State
    - Heads of State Departments
  - State Auditor
  - State Treasurer

—— elected
----- appointed

Legislative Branch

- Senate
- House of Representatives

Judicial Branch

- Supreme Court
- Court of Appeals
- Circuit Courts
- Superior Courts

The Judicial Branch

Indiana's court system makes up the judicial branch of state government. The job of the courts is to apply state laws in deciding whether or not someone has broken the law.

At the top level of the court system is the state supreme court. It consists of a chief justice and four associate justices. A judicial commission selects one of the five supreme court judges to serve as chief justice for the next five years.

Indiana's counties

Dan Quayle

James Danforth Quayle was born in Indianapolis in 1947. He served as vice president under Republican president George Bush from 1989 to 1993. Quayle graduated from DePauw University in 1969 and received his law degree from Indiana University in 1974. He represented Indiana in the U.S. House of Representatives from 1977 to 1981 and in the Senate from then until 1989. Quayle is a political conservative. His memoir, *Standing Firm,* came out in 1994. ■

At the next level is the state court of appeals. Its twelve judges preside over courts in the state's five judicial districts. One of the appeals judges rules over a tax court. When there's an opening on the supreme court or the appeals court, the governor appoints a judge to that position. Then in the next election, voters vote on the appointment. If the judge is approved, he or she serves a ten-year term.

Richard Lugar

Republican Richard G. Lugar has represented Indiana in the U.S. Senate since 1977. He was born in Indianapolis in 1932 and attended public schools there. As a college student, he became a Rhodes scholar, studying at Pembroke College in Oxford, England. Lugar served as mayor of Indianapolis from 1968 to 1975. In 1972, he delivered the keynote address at the Republican National Convention. He was elected to the U.S. Senate in 1976, where he served as a member of the Senate Intelligence Committee and the Senate Foreign Relations Committee. ▪

The third level of courts are Indiana's ninety circuit courts. Each court presides over one county—with two exceptions. Jefferson and Switzerland Counties are combined into one judicial circuit, and Dearborn and Ohio Counties are joined, too. Some counties also have superior courts or various special courts.

Local Government

Indiana is divided into ninety-two counties. All but one are governed by a three-member board of county commissioners. Voters elect the commissioners to four-year terms. In Marion County and Indianapolis, voters elect a mayor and twenty-nine council members.

Within the counties are cities, towns, and townships. Cities are governed by a mayor and a city council, while towns have town councils. In townships, voters elect a township trustee to serve a four-year term.

CHAPTER EIGHT

Hoosiers at Work

Some Indiana farms raise ostriches in addition to other livestock.

Not many people know that ostriches and llamas are among Indiana's barnyard animals. About 7,000 ostriches and 1,500 llamas thrive on its farms. Ostriches are prized for their meat. It's low in fat and cholesterol and high in protein and iron. Llama fleece is much softer than sheep's wool.

Livestock farmers also raise chickens, turkeys, pigs, beef and milk cattle, and sheep. Indiana is the nation's number-one duck producer. It supplies almost one-third of the country's ducks. Hogs are the state's most valuable livestock animal though.

Milk and ice cream are some of the state's main dairy products. Indiana is second in the country in ice-cream production. It's also a top egg-producing state.

In overall farm income, Indiana ranks in the top one-fourth of the nation. More than 70 percent of the state is farmland, with the richest soil in the central plains. In the late 1990s, there were about 63,000 farms in Indiana. As in other states, the number of farms has gone down over the years. But, thanks to better and faster machinery, the shrinking number of farms are producing more crops than ever.

Corn and soybeans bring in the most money, and they're grown in every county. Together, these two crops account for about half of the state's farm income every year.

Opposite: A soybean farm in Shelby County

Mama, Let's Get a Llama!

According to their owners, llamas are much more than just farm animals. Marilyn Nenni, owner of Shagbark Ridge Llamas in Noblesville, claims that llamas are "something the entire family can work on, from grandma to the four-year-old." Like cats and dogs, they make great companions too. Tom Riley, former president of the Hoosier Llama Association, says, "You can hike with them, pack with them. You just love them, and they'll love you back." ■

Many kinds of corn grow in Indiana, including corn for animal feed, sweet corn for humans, and popcorn. In fact, in 1997, Indiana ranked first in the nation in popcorn production, growing more than 20 percent of all the popcorn in the country.

Other valuable crops are grains such as wheat, oats, and rye; and vegetables such as tomatoes, snap beans, and cucumbers. Important fruit crops include cantaloupes, watermelons, blueberries, apples, and peaches. Indiana farmers also grow tobacco, hay, and the savory herbs we enjoy in chewing gum—peppermint and spearmint. These herbs thrive in the marshy soil of the northeastern lake country.

Manufacturing

Manufacturing is Indiana's most important industry and the state's biggest employer. The major industrial cities are clustered in the Calumet region of northwest Indiana, along Lake Michigan. They include Gary, Hammond, East Chicago, Burns Harbor, and Whiting.

Cars, trucks, and other transportation equipment are Indiana's

Grilled Corn on the Cob

Grilled corn on the cob is a traditional summer snack or side dish in the Midwest.

Ingredients:

 1 dozen ears corn
 salty water
 butter

Directions:

Slowly strip back the husks of each ear of corn, exposing the silks. Remove all of the silk, then pull the husks back over the ear so that it is completely covered. Place the ears in a large bowl, pot, or bucket of salty water and soak them overnight, or all day.

Ask an adult to prepare an outdoor grill. Place the corn directly on the grill. Grill for a few minutes, until the corn inside the husks is tender and hot.

Serve with softened butter.

Serves 6.

most important factory goods. Factories in Fort Wayne, Kokomo, Indianapolis, and Columbus make parts for motor vehicles and airplanes. Plants in Elkhart, Fort Wayne, and Lafayette assemble automotive parts into ready-for-the-road vehicles. Hammond makes both petroleum products and railroad equipment.

What Indiana Grows, Manufactures, and Mines

Agriculture	Manufacturing	Mining
Corn	Chemicals	Coal
Hogs	Electrical equipment	Limestone
Soybeans	Food products	
	Machinery	
	Primary metals	
	Transportation equipment	

Metals are next in importance among Indiana's manufactured goods. When U.S. Steel began production at its plant in Gary in early 1909, it was the largest steel mill in the world. Today, Indiana is the top steel-producing state and one of the world's leading steel centers. Gary and East Chicago are the major steel cities. Aluminum is another important metal, with manufacturing centers in Bedford, Lafayette, and Newburgh.

Indiana is a leading producer of chemicals, and drugs are its most important chemical product. These range from simple, over-the-counter medications such as aspirin to complex prescription drugs. Indianapolis is the headquarters for the massive Eli Lilly and Company drug firm. Elkhart and Evansville also manufacture drugs. Industrial plants in Whiting make chemicals and soaps, as well as petroleum products.

Food products from Indiana include soft drinks and delicious bakery goods. And Elkhart is known the world over as a source for fine musical instruments. Electronic and electrical equipment, industrial machinery, and rubber and plastic products are among Indiana's many other factory goods.

Minerals and Mining

Coal is the state's number-one mineral. Most of it comes from strip mines in southwestern Indiana. In the same region, oil wells pump raw petroleum from deep beneath the surface of the earth.

Limestone quarries in south-central Indiana supply huge chunks of stone for constructing buildings. The Empire State Building in New York City and the Pentagon near Washington,

The Eli Lilly and Company headquarters in Indianapolis

Chicago
Lake Michigan
MICHIGAN
South Bend
Gary
Kankakee
Maumee
Fort Wayne
N
OHIO
Wabash
ILLINOIS
Indianapolis
Miami
White
Cincinnati
Ohio
Kentucky
Wabash
White
Louisville
0 40 mi.
0 40 km
Evansville
KENTUCKY
Farming
Forests, some farming
Urban or industrial area
Cattle
Chemicals
Clay
Coal
Corn
Dairy
Fruit
Gypsum
Hay
Hogs
Limestone
Manufacturing
Melons
Natural gas
Oats
Petroleum
Potatoes
Poultry
Rye
Sheep
Soybeans
Tobacco
Vegetables
Wheat

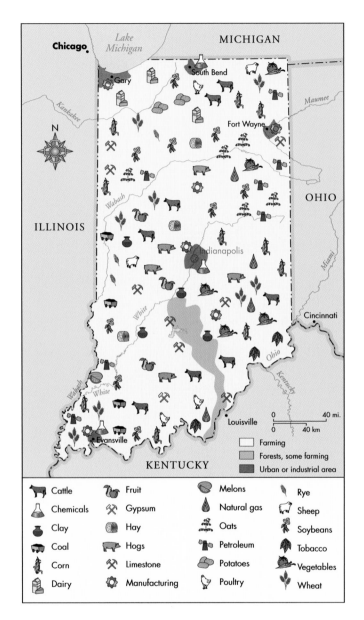

Indiana's natural resources

D.C., are among the famous buildings made out of Indiana limestone. Crushed limestone is good for making concrete and building highways. Sand, gravel, clay, and gypsum are some of Indiana's other valuable minerals.

Main Street of the Midwest

Indiana likes to call itself the Main Street of the Midwest, and it's easy to see why. Thirteen interstate highways cross Indiana—more than any other state. Several of these highways run through Indianapolis, a major crossroads for the midwestern United States. Indiana had a national "main street" back in the early 1880s. The National Road, or Cumberland Road, was Indiana's first interstate highway. Now it's Route 40. Indiana is an important rail center too. All railroad lines that run east from Chicago, Illinois, and St. Louis, Missouri, go through Indiana.

International air passengers don't need to change planes when they travel in and out of Indiana. The Indianapolis International Airport provides service to dozens of cities around the world. It's

Indiana's largest airport. Airports in South Bend and Fort Wayne are the next busiest.

The state has three international ports. The largest is Burns Harbor at Portage on Lake Michigan. Every ship that arrives there has traveled a long way. From the Atlantic Ocean, ships enter the St. Lawrence Seaway and make their way through the Great Lakes—Ontario, Erie, and Huron—and travel the length of Lake Michigan to Burns Harbor. The state's other ports, Clark Maritime Center and Southwind Maritime Center, are on the Ohio River.

Freighters and barges on Lake Superior and Lake Michigan bring iron ore, coal, and other minerals from Minnesota and Michi-

The Indianapolis International Airport serves Hoosiers with flights all over the world.

Burns Harbor on Lake Michigan

gan. The iron goes directly to the steel mills along the lake. River traffic is just as busy. More freight travels on the Ohio River than passes through the Panama Canal.

Getting the Word Out

Have you ever heard of the *Coon-Skinner,* the *Broad Axe of Freedom,* or the *Grubbing Hoe of Truth*? You might have if you had been a Hoosier pioneer. They were some of Indiana's earliest newspapers.

Pioneer newspaper editors had a down-home sense of humor, but they also made heroic efforts to get the word out. Many came into a new town lugging their own printing presses. They did all their own reporting, writing, printing, and distribution. And most had to hold other jobs to make ends meet. They often had to skip issues because they were in such dire financial straits.

One hard-luck tale involved the editor of the *Dog-Fennel Gazette* of Rushville. He was so hard up for money that he printed his paper on one side of a sheet of paper. When he passed it out to readers, he asked that they return it when they had read it so that he could print the next issue on the other side!

Elihu Stout published Indiana's first newspaper, the *Indiana Gazette*, in Vincennes in 1804. Like most pioneer newspapers, it came out once a week. The first daily papers were the *Journal* and the *Sentinel.* Both started publication in Indianapolis in 1851. The

Journal is now the *Indianapolis Star,* the largest newspaper in the state. Statewide, more than 250 newspapers are published, and about 60 of them are daily papers.

WSBT, Indiana's first radio station, was established by the *South Bend Tribune* in 1921. Television broadcasting arrived in 1949, when two stations hit the airwaves: Bloomington's WTTV and Indianapolis's WFBM. WFBM is now called WRTV. Along with about 33 other stations, 45 cable broadcasters, and 170 radio stations, they're getting the word out as faithfully as the pioneer newspeople did.

The Indianapolis Star

From Dummies to Complete Idiots

First there was *DOS for Dummies.* Then there was *The Complete Idiot's Guide to Personal Computers.* Before long, Indiana was the computer-book-publishing capital of the world. The *Dummies* books now number more than 350 titles on subjects from computers to classical music.

Complete Idiot's guides cover everything from the Internet to dating. Publishers of these wildly popular manuals are located in the Indianapolis area. IDG Books Worldwide publishes the *Dummies* line, and Alpha, a division of Macmillan Publishing USA, produces the *Complete Idiot's* series. ■

CHAPTER NINE

People Who Make a Difference

Some Hoosiers still have a rural way of life.

t's fascinating to see how Indiana has grown over the last two centuries. A population count in 1800 found only 5,641 people in what is now Indiana! By 1860, the state's population had grown to 1,350,428—the fifth-highest in the country. Today, more than 5.5 million people live in Indiana. While the state has continued to grow, other states have grown faster. Indiana is now the fourteenth-largest state in the nation.

Where People Live

If Hoosiers spread themselves out so that they were evenly spaced across the whole state, there would be about 154 people living on every square mile (59 per sq km). That much space would give every man, woman, and child in the state 3.8 football fields of their very own!

Opposite: Showing off the top prize at the Owen County Fair

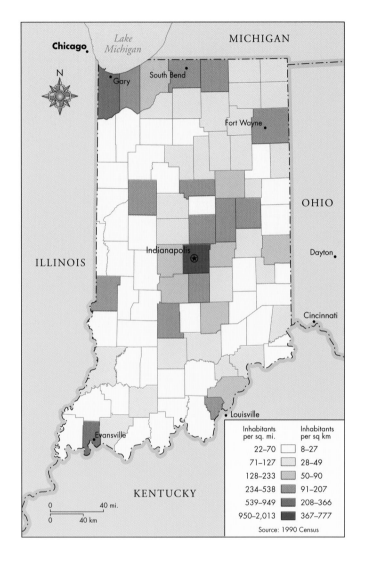

Indiana's population density

It's been a long time since Hoosiers were spread that far apart though. In 1860, fewer than one-tenth of the people in Indiana lived in cities. Many settlers lived miles from their nearest neighbors. Most people lived in the southern part of the state at that time.

As heavy industry grew, the settlement pattern shifted to the north. Today, more than two-thirds of the population live in urban areas, and most of the people and the large cities are in the northern half of the state. About one-third of all Indiana residents live in the Indianapolis and Gary metropolitan areas.

The Largest Cities

Indianapolis, the capital and largest city, is located right in the center of the state. Almost three-quarters of a million people live there. The city is Indiana's financial and cultural center, and the headquarters of many large corporations.

The Calumet region along Lake Michigan is one of the nation's top steel-producing areas. It includes such industrial cities as Gary, East Chicago, Whiting, Hammond, and Michigan City. While the whole region is a dense population center, Gary is the only one of these cities with more than 100,000 residents. It's Indiana's fourth-largest city, while Hammond ranks number six.

Fort Wayne, in the northeast, is the second-largest city in the state. It started out as a French fur-trading post in 1680 and is now an important railroad and manufacturing center. Evansville, the third-largest city, sits on the Ohio River in the far southwest. The north-central city of South Bend ranks fifth in size.

South Bend is one of the state's largest cities.

The people of Indiana come from many different backgrounds.

Where Did Everyone Come From?

Hoosiers' ancestors came from all over the globe. Most of Indiana's early pioneers were descended from English, Scottish, and Welsh people. The first big wave of settlers came from the South and made their homes in southern Indiana. Even today, people in the southern part of the state have a gentle but distinct southern drawl. Later arrivals settled in the north, coming from New York, Pennsylvania, and other eastern states.

Many immigrants from Germany and Ireland arrived in the mid-1800s. As steel mills and other heavy industries expanded, they attracted thousands of newcomers from Poland, Hungary, Belgium, and Italy. African-Americans from the South were drawn to the northern industrial cities too.

Descendants of all these ethnic groups are found in almost every part of Indiana today. But some groups are more prominent in certain cities and regions. People of Polish ancestry, for instance, make up much of South Bend's population. Descendants of Hungarians, Belgians, and Italians are dominant across northern Indiana. About 70 percent of the people in Gary, 30 percent of East Chicagoans, and 20 percent of Indianapolis's people are African-Americans.

Only a small percentage of Indiana's residents today are immigrants. They came from Mexico, Canada, Germany, Great Britain, and Southeast Asia.

Indiana was a safe haven for various religious groups in the pioneer days. One group was the Society of Friends, also called Quakers. They arrived around 1807 and established a community in Richmond. Simple and devout, they held their religious services in plain, undecorated meetinghouses. They valued education highly and opened Earlham College in 1847.

Amish and Mennonite people from Germany and Switzerland arrived in the early 1800s. Most of them settled in the northeastern counties, where they still thrive. Called the "plain people," they believe in living simply and peacefully, without the distractions of modern technology. They live

Population of Indiana's Major Cities (1990)

Indianapolis	731,327
Fort Wayne	173,072
Evansville	126,272
Gary	116,646
South Bend	105,511
Hammond	84,236

Many Amish live in Indiana.

in farming communities, wear plain, dark clothing, and use no electricity, telephones, or cars.

From Wilderness Schools to the Big Ten

It wasn't easy to trudge through the snow to a one-room log schoolhouse. But Hoosiers valued education, and they did whatever it took to get one. Indiana's 1816 constitution was the first in the nation to call for free public schools, but the state couldn't provide the money to build these schools until the 1850s. In the meantime, parents took matters into their own hands. They built their own schools and paid what they could scrape together for tuition.

Later, Robert Owen and his New Harmony community introduced many experiments in education that were radical at the time. They included nursery schools, trade schools, coeducational classes, and teaching by stimulating the students' interest. By now, all these ideas seem rather normal!

It was not until 1879 that Indiana required all school-age children to attend classes. Even then, the students were required to be in school for only twelve weeks of the year. Today, children between seven and fifteen years of age must attend school—and the school year is quite a bit longer. Besides its public schools, Indiana has several nationally known private schools, such as Howe and Culver military academies.

Religious groups founded some of Indiana's earliest colleges, and many of them are still open today. Presbyterians established Hanover College in Madison in 1827 and Wabash College in Crawfordsville in 1832. Methodists opened today's DePauw University in Greencastle in 1837. Catholics founded Notre Dame University

Students at Hanover College

Notre Dame University was founded as a Catholic college.

near South Bend in 1842. Today it is one of the top Catholic universities in the world. Baptists founded Franklin College in 1834 and Indianapolis's Butler University in 1855. And Earlham College in Richmond began as a Quaker school in 1847.

Today, more than half of Indiana's college students attend one of the state-supported public universities. The largest are Purdue

University in West Lafayette and Indiana University (IU) in Bloomington. Both have several regional campuses around the state.

Purdue has the top enrollment in the country in its undergraduate engineering programs. Both Purdue and IU are Big Ten schools in college athletics. More medical doctors graduate from IU than from any other school in the nation, and its music school is one of the best in the country. Indiana State University in Terre Haute, Ball State University in Muncie, Vincennes University in Vincennes, and the University of Southern Indiana in Evansville are Indiana's other public universities.

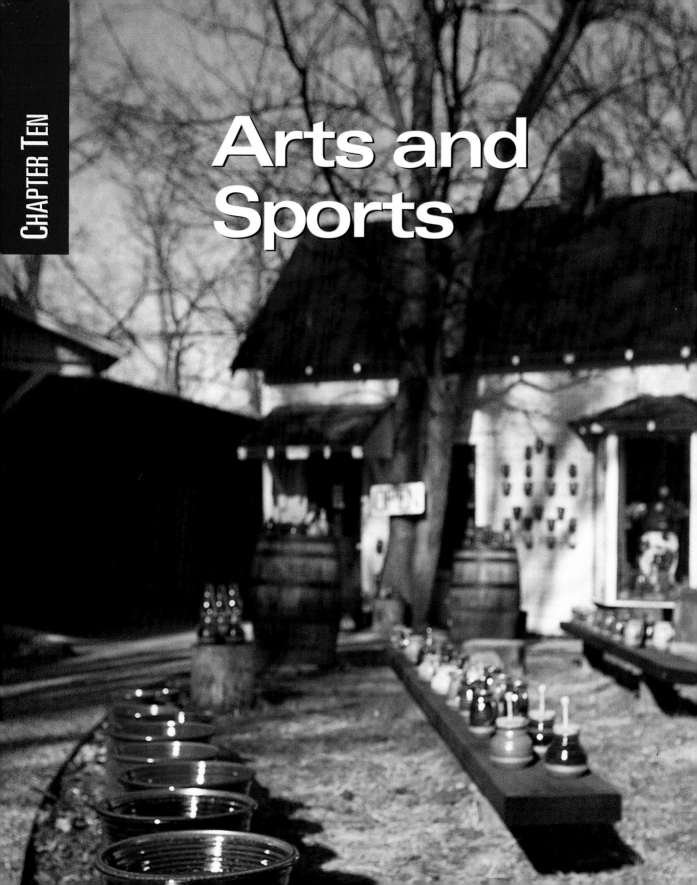

CHAPTER TEN

Arts and Sports

ndianapolis-born comedian David Letterman is no ordinary talk-show host. With his zany comedy and irreverent style, his *Late Show with David Letterman* appeals to a young TV audience like no other nightly show. Letterman is quick to honor his Hoosier roots—and his mother, whom he has featured on the show now and then.

David Letterman (right) with his mom (left) and bandleader Paul Shaffer

Indiana seems to be a breeding ground for popular entertainers. Comedians Red Skelton and Herb Shriner were both Hoosiers, and so were actors James Dean and Steve McQueen. Composer Cole Porter gave the world such unforgettable songs as "Night and Day" and "I've Got You under My Skin." Another Hoosier, pianist Hoagy Carmichael, wrote "Georgia on My Mind" as well as "Star Dust"—one of the most popular songs of the 1930s and 1940s.

A more recent entertainer to come out of Indiana is superstar Michael Jackson. Born in Gary in 1958, the singer, dancer, and songwriter is one the best-selling record and concert artists of all time.

John "Cougar" Mellencamp of Seymour topped the charts with his 1980s hit singles "Jack and Diane" and "Hurts So Good." In the years that followed, Mellencamp earned dozens of gold and platinum record-industry awards. Where did the name "Cougar"

Opposite: A pottery shop in Nashville

John Mellencamp is a singer from the Hoosier State.

come from? Mellencamp's producer put the name "Johnny Cougar" on one of his early albums. Mellencamp got the shock of his life when the album came out. He had no idea that the producer had planned to change his name!

Another Hoosier entertainer—in quite a different field—is TV anchorwoman Jane Pauley. A native of Indianapolis, she's the award-winning host of the news show *Dateline NBC*.

Cultural performing arts are alive and well in Indiana too. The highly respected Indianapolis Symphony Orchestra performs in Hilbert Circle Theatre. The Civic Theater there is the oldest continuously operating theater in the country. South Bend, Fort Wayne, and other smaller cities support their own symphony orchestras. People who live in college towns can enjoy the schools' many musical offerings. Butler University's Clowes Hall features its own symphony orchestra, as well as touring musicals.

Twyla Tharp

Dancer and choreographer Twyla Tharp was born in Portland in 1941. An acclaimed innovator in modern dance, Tharp blends music and dance elements together in bold new ways. Her choreography is a mixture of classical ballet, tap dance, and popular social dances. The musical accompaniment is just as diverse, merging classical music, jazz, and rock and roll. ∎

Cole Porter

Cole Albert Porter (1891–1964) was born into a wealthy family in Peru, Indiana. His musical talent was apparent when he was very young, and he published his first song at age eleven. Porter graduated from Yale University, studied law for a short time, and then switched his efforts to music. For more than forty years he composed a contin-uous stream of elegant, witty, artistic songs for Broadway and film musicals. A *very* short list of his hit songs includes "Night and Day," "I've Got You under My Skin," "Begin the Beguine," "I Love Paris," and "My Heart Belongs to Daddy." Among Porter's musicals are *High Society, Can-Can, Silk Stockings,* and *Kiss Me, Kate.* ■

Author! Author!

More great writers have come out of Indiana than from any other state of its size. How did this happen? Nobody knows for sure. One person's bright suggestion was, "Maybe it's something in the water"! It would be hard to name all the notable poets, novelists, and playwrights in Indiana's literary history, but here are some of the stars.

James Whitcomb Riley

Poet James Whitcomb Riley (1849–1916) was born in Green-field. Leaving school at sixteen, he traveled the Indiana countryside painting houses and signs. He published his first poems while working for the Greenfield news-paper. Riley became associate edi-tor of the *Anderson Democrat* but was fired for claiming a poem by Edgar Allan Poe was his own. After Riley joined the staff of the *Indianapolis Journal,* his poetry began to be popular all over the country. Some of his best-loved poems are "Little Orphant Annie" and "When the Frost Is on the Punkin." ■

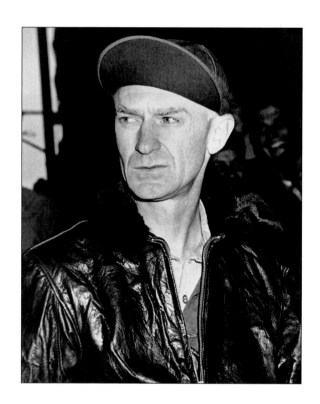

Ernie Pyle was a journalist during World War II.

James Whitcomb Riley was known as the Hoosier Poet. He loved Indiana folklore and Indiana folks, and he used the Indiana country dialect in many of his lovingly written poems.

Booth Tarkington, born in Indianapolis, gave his stories a midwestern setting. *The Gentleman from Indiana* is one of his most popular tales. Two of Tarkington's novels—*The Magnificent Ambersons* and *Alice Adams*—won Pulitzer Prizes for fiction.

Journalist Ernie Pyle showed America what life was like in the trenches during World War II. He won a 1944 Pulitzer Prize for his stirring reports from the field. As a war correspondent, Pyle believed in getting close to his subject—a belief that eventually cost him his life. He was killed in action during the Okinawa campaign.

Humorist George Ade of Kentland loved to poke fun at people in his stories and plays. His comedy opera *The Sultan of Sulu* was a Broadway hit. Rex Stout of Noblesville is famous for his detective novels featuring Nero Wolfe.

Novelist Theodore Dreiser of Terre Haute wrote *Sister Carrie* and *An American Tragedy*. Many of Dreiser's tragic characters are victims of a cruel and thoughtless society. Lew Wallace is most famous for his novel *Ben-Hur*, which was made into a blockbuster epic movie.

Novelist Jessamyn West portrayed the struggles of an Indiana Quaker family during the Civil War in her novel *The Friendly Persuasion*. Brilliant and offbeat, the novelist Kurt Vonnegut has produced *Slaughterhouse Five* and dozens of other popular stories.

Museums Galore

Indianapolis offers a wonderland of artistic and cultural museums. Collections in the Indianapolis Museum of Art represent thousands of years' worth of paintings and decorative objects. The Indiana State Museum highlights the state's history, geography, and art. The Children's Museum in Indianapolis is the world's largest museum devoted to kids.

For a fascinating glimpse of Native American culture, there is the Eiteljorg Museum of American Indians and Western Art. Abraham Lincoln memorabilia is the focus of the Lincoln Library and Museum in Fort Wayne. It's full of photos, paintings, and books relating to the beloved president who spent his early years in Indiana.

Indiana University's art museum is world famous, and Valparaiso University operates an impressive Center for the Arts. Evansville, Fort Wayne, Terre Haute, South Bend, and Notre Dame University all have impressive art museums. Rock star

Jessamyn West wrote about an Indiana Quaker family in *The Friendly Persuasion*.

The Children's Museum in Indianapolis

John Mellencamp donated his private art collection to the Southern Indiana Center for the Arts in his hometown of Seymour.

Indiana artist Theodore Clement (T. C.) Steele lived in Nashville. When he built his home there in 1907, he named it the House of the Singing Winds. Now one of the nation's most famous art colonies flourishes in this southern Indiana community. Attracted by the region's scenic beauty, artists such as Steele began to gather there almost a century ago. Nashville's art galleries are open all year, and actors from Indiana University stage plays in Nashville's theater.

Racing fans are drawn to the Indy 500 at the Indianapolis Motor Speedway.

The Indy 500

The massive crowd shuffles in anticipation. Hundreds of thousands of people try to contain their excitement and stay quiet so that they can hear the magical words. The loudspeakers boom: "Gentlemen and ladies, start your engines!" And then it's hard to tell which is louder—the roar of the crowd or the dozens of car engines revving up.

It's race day at the Indianapolis Motor Speedway, time for the Indianapolis 500. Not only is this Memorial Day weekend race the biggest and most-popular challenge on the international auto-racing calendar, it's the biggest day of the year in Indiana. Thousands

The Brickyard

Built in 1909 from 3,200,000 paving bricks, the Indianapolis Motor Speedway has hosted an annual 500-mile (805-km) race every year beginning in 1911. At a distance of 2.5 miles (4 km) around the track, it takes 200 laps to complete the grueling race. ■

upon thousands of people converge on the city from all over the world. Many come in campers and make a two-week festival out of the event—from the time trials through the race itself. With seating for more than 250,000 people (and room for thousands more on the infield), the speedway becomes a city unto itself. There is even an adjacent golf course with eighteen holes actually placed inside and around the racecourse!

Besides attracting millions of race fans, the Indy 500 draws the world's top auto racers. A. J. Foyt, Rick Mears, and Al Unser Sr. have each won the race four times, and each man is a legend in the world of auto racing. With a prize purse of more than $8 million, who wouldn't want to race at Indianapolis?

In 1994, the NASCAR Brickyard 400 was run at the Speedway for the first time. Hoosier Jeff Gordon has won it twice.

Hoosier Hoops

Although basketball is often called the "city game," Indiana rightly calls itself the home of basketball. Nowhere else in the United States is the game played or watched more passionately. From youth leagues through high school, college, and the NBA, the basketball season is as important in Indiana as winter, spring, summer, and fall.

Surely, the hotbed of Indiana basketball is Assembly Hall at the Bloomington campus of Indiana University. With every fan decked out in red and white, an Indiana Hoosiers game is a sight to behold. IU has won the NCAA men's basketball championship five times (1940, 1953, 1976, 1981, and 1987) and the Big Ten Conference title nearly twenty times. Coached by the fiery Hall of Famer Bob

Indiana's Luke Recker (right)

Knight since 1971, Indiana's teams have always been known for an intense, competitive spirit that matches their coach's demeanor.

"Hoosier Hysteria"—or basketball fever—hits high schools all over the state at tournament time. Indiana is loaded with powerhouse teams, but everyone remembers the "Milan Miracle" of 1954, when an unknown team from Milan High School defeated the mighty Muncie Central team for the state championship. This classic underdog story was immortalized in the 1987 film *Hoosiers*.

Coach Bob Knight is known for his temper as well as his success.

The Fighting Irish

Yet another national sports legend resides in Indiana. When most Americans think of college football, one of the first schools that comes to mind is the University of Notre Dame. Back in 1913, a pass receiver named Knute Rockne single-handedly revolutionized college football by making the passing game a highly potent scoring weapon. In the 1920s, when he was Notre Dame's head coach, Rockne's name became synonymous with winning: from 1918 to

"Larry Legend"

Nobody would call him the biggest, strongest, or fastest player on the court, but in just about every game he played, Larry Bird was the best. Bird's legend began in the middle of Indiana's corn country in the small town of French Lick. Bird began grabbing statewide headlines at Springs Valley High School, and he later put Indiana State University on the basketball map with his phenomenal senior season of 1978–1979. The ISU Sycamores went into the 1979 NCAA championship game as an undefeated team, but despite Bird's heroics, they came out losers to Michigan State, led by Earvin "Magic" Johnson. The Bird-Johnson showdown has been called a classic, and the two players' spectacular rivalry continued for more than a decade in the NBA.

In his thirteen-year pro career, Bird led the Boston Celtics to three NBA titles, and many times in the 1980s, he faced Magic Johnson's Los Angeles Lakers in classic NBA finals duels. Bird was adored by Boston fans for his uncanny last-second baskets and steals, and his incredible ability to play through back and foot injuries that dogged him throughout his career.

In 1997, Bird returned home as head coach (above) of the NBA's Indiana Pacers, immediately revitalizing and inspiring a team that had been floundering in recent seasons. "Larry Legend" was inducted into the Naismith Memorial Basketball Hall of Fame in 1998. ▪

The Four Horsemen

1930, Notre Dame posted an incredible record of 105 wins, 12 losses, and 5 ties. Rockne was a football innovator in every way—from game strategy to scheduling games and even to marketing. In 1924, sportswriter Grantland Rice borrowed a biblical image and nicknamed ND's all-American backfield the Four Horsemen. By this time, this was just one more page in the legend of Notre Dame football. And as the winning continued year after year, the Fighting Irish fable only deepened. Since World War II, the school has won eight national football championships.

Over the years, the Fighting Irish have been the source of plenty of legends, lore, and famous quotes—whether real or fictional. Coach Knute Rockne is supposed to have said, "I found prayers work best when you have big players." And George Gipp, a Notre Dame star of the 1920s, gave a young actor named Ronald Reagan his most famous line. Playing Gipp in the 1940 movie *Knute Rockne: All American*, Reagan tugged on the nation's heart strings when he uttered Gipp's deathbed entreaty: "Let's win one for the Gipper!"

It's been said that Hoosiers are more focused on local interests than they are on national or world affairs. But it's plain to see that Hoosiers have plenty to be proud of—whether it's their championship sports teams, their industrial know-how, or their many home-grown artists, writers, and political leaders. Beneath the Hoosier pride is a strong sense of who they are and of the courage and dedication it took to get where they are today.

Mark Spitz

The greatest Olympic swimmer of all time, Mark Spitz, is a Hoosier native. Spitz captured a record seven gold medals at the 1972 Olympic Games. ∎

Timeline

United States History

The first permanent English settlement is established in North America at Jamestown. **1607**

Pilgrims found Plymouth Colony, the second permanent English settlement. **1620**

America declares its independence from Britain. **1776**

The Treaty of Paris officially ends the Revolutionary War in America. **1783**

The U.S. Constitution is written. **1787**

The Louisiana Purchase almost doubles the size of the United States. **1803**

The United States and Britain **1812–15** fight the War of 1812.

Indiana State History

1679 René-Robert Cavelier, Sieur de La Salle, sails into the St. Joseph River, becoming the first European to arrive in what is now Indiana.

1732 Jesuit missionaries found Vincennes, the first permanent settlement in Indiana.

1754–1763 The French and Indian War erupts. It ends with the Treaty of Paris, in which France gives Britain all the land east of the Mississippi River, including what is now Indiana.

1787 Under the Northwest Ordinance, Indiana becomes part of the Northwest Territory.

1800 Indiana Territory is established.

1816 Indiana becomes the nineteenth state on December 11.

1825 Indianapolis becomes the state's new capital after Indian land in central Indiana is bought back.

United States History

The North and South fight **1861–65** each other in the American Civil War.

The United States is **1917–18** involved in World War I.

The stock market crashes, **1929** plunging the United States into the Great Depression.

The United States **1941–45** fights in World War II.

The United States becomes a **1945** charter member of the U.N.

The United States **1951–53** fights in the Korean War.

The U.S. Congress enacts a series of **1964** groundbreaking civil rights laws.

The United States **1964–73** engages in the Vietnam War.

The United States and other **1991** nations fight the brief Persian Gulf War against Iraq.

Indiana State History

1820s The state begins building of roads and canals.

1889 One of the largest oil refineries in the world is built in Whiting by the Standard Oil Company.

1906 U.S. Steel lays out plans to build Gary as an adjunct to its steel-making plants that begin production in January 1909.

1911 The first Indianapolis 500 race event is held.

1930s Farms fail after World War I and the crash of the stock market.

1956 The Indiana Toll Road joins the western and eastern borders of the state.

1970 The Port of Indiana opens.

1988 The state lottery is established.

Fast Facts

State capitol

Cardinal

Statehood date	December 11, 1816, the 19th state
Origin of state name	Latin for "land of the Indians"
State capital	Indianapolis
State nickname	Hoosier State
State motto	"The Crossroads of America"
State bird	Cardinal
State flower	Peony
State rock	Limestone
State tree	Tulip tree (yellow poplar)
State song	"On the Banks of the Wabash, Far Away"
State fair	Indianapolis (mid-August)

Wabash River

Total area; rank	36,420 sq. mi. (94,328 sq km); 38th
Land; rank	35,870 sq. mi. (92,903 sq km); 38th
Water; rank	550 sq. mi. (1,425 sq km); 38th
***Inland water;* rank**	315 sq. mi. (816 sq km); 42nd
***Great Lakes water;* rank**	235 sq. mi. (608 sq km); 8th
Geographic center	Boone, 14 miles (23 km) northwest of Indianapolis
Latitude and longitude	Indiana is located approximately between 37° 47' and 41° 46' N and 84° 49' and 88° 02' W
Highest point	In Wayne County, 1,257 feet (383 m) above sea level
Lowest point	In Posey County, 320 feet (98 m) above sea level
Largest city	Indianapolis
Number of counties	92
Population; rank	5,564,228 (1990 census); 14th
Density	154 persons per sq. mi. (59 per sq km)
Population distribution	65% urban, 35% rural

Ethnic distribution (does not equal 100%)

White	90.56%
African-American	7.79%
Hispanic	1.78%
Asian and Pacific Islanders	0.68%
Native American	0.23%
Other	0.74%

Young Hoosiers

Record high temperature	116°F (47°C) at Collegeville on July 14, 1936
Record low temperature	–35°F (–37°C) at Greensburg on February 2, 1951
Average July temperature	75°F (24°C)
Average January temperature	28°F (–2°C)
Average annual precipitation	40 inches (102 cm)

Natural Areas and Historic Sites

National Lakeshores
Indiana Dunes National Lakeshore is on the southern shore of Lake Michigan and includes a working farm from the early 1900s, a French-Canadian homestead, and different types of landforms for those interested in the environment.

National Historical Parks
George Rogers Clark National Historical Park is the site of Fort Sackville, where Lieutenant Colonel George Rogers Clark of the Continental army captured the fort from British Lieutenant Governor Henry Hamilton during the Revolutionary War.

National Memorials
Lincoln Boyhood National Memorial is the site of Abraham Lincoln's home for fourteen years. Other features include the burial site of President Lincoln's mother, a visitor center, and a rebuilt living pioneer homestead.

George Rogers Clark National Historic Park

Hoosier National Forest

National Forests

Hoosier National Forest in southern Indiana covers 195,000 acres (79,000 ha). It includes various smaller sites, including the Pioneer Mothers Memorial Forest, an old-growth forest; Hemlock Cliffs, which overlook a sandstone canyon; and Hickory Ridge Lookout Tower, which is listed on the National Historic Lookout Register.

State Parks

Indiana has twenty-three state parks. At Tippecanoe River State Park, which includes Bass Lake State Beach, outdoor enthusiasts can canoe down the Tippecanoe River as well as fish in its waters or hike along its trails. Clifty Falls State Park, in Madison, allows visitors to enjoy the Ohio River valley, providing gorgeous views of waterfalls, a canyon, and the city of Madison. Harmonie State Park, in New Harmony, allows history lovers to see the nineteenth-century experimental town as well as a beautiful landscape.

Sports Teams

Hoosier basketball

NCAA Teams (Division 1)

Ball State University Cardinals

Butler University Sycamores

Indiana University-Bloomington Hoosiers

Purdue University Boilermakers

University of Evansville Aces

University of Notre Dame Fighting Irish

Valparaiso University Crusaders

National Basketball Association

Indiana Pacers

National Football League

Indianapolis Colts

Children's Museum

Cultural Institutions

Libraries

The Indiana State Library has information on the history of the state and its citizens, along with genealogical records for family history research.

The Indiana University–Purdue University at Indianapolis Library includes a special philanthropic library as well as government statistics, information on the state, and general collections.

The Willard Library in Evansville is Indiana's oldest public library building, opened in the late nineteenth century. Its Victorian Gothic walls hold the Thrall Art Book Collection and a rich supply of genealogical resources.

Museums

The Children's Museum (Indianapolis) is the world's largest museum devoted to kids.

The Great Lakes Museum of Military History in Michigan City contains rare documents, old military uniforms, medals, and weapons used in combat.

The Indiana Railway Museum in French Lick gives train rides through parts of Hoosier National Forest, moving through Burton Tunnel, one of the longest railroad tunnels in Indiana.

The Indiana State Museum in Indianapolis contains a wealth of information on the state, such as radio and television broadcast history, sports history, and prehistoric exhibits.

The Indianapolis Museum of Art is the seventh-largest nonspecialized art museum in the United States. It has many collections, including Chinese, neo-impressionist, and African artwork. Lush museum gardens surround the museum.

Performing Arts

Indiana has one major opera company, two major symphony orchestras, and one major dance company.

Indiana University

Universities and Colleges

In the mid-1990s, Indiana had forty-nine public and twenty-eight private institutions of higher learning.

Annual Events

January–March
Winter sports in Laporte and New Carlisle (January and February)

Parke County Maple Fair in Rockville (February–March)

Indiana High School Athletic Association State Basketball Tournament in Indianapolis (March)

April–June
Sugar Creek Canoe Race in Crawfordsville (April)

Marion Easter Pageant (April or May)

Tulipfest in Bloomington (April)

Mushroom Festival in Mansfield (April)

Indianapolis 500 race and festival (Memorial Day weekend)

Bluegrass Music Festival in Beanblossom (June)

Glass Festival in Greentown (June)

Festival of the Arts and Crafts in Lowell (June)

Miss Indiana Pageant in Michigan City (June)

July–September
Freedom Festival in Evansville (June and July)

Circus City Festival in Peru (July)

Hydroplane Regatta in Madison (July)

Indiana State Fair in Indianapolis (August)

National Muzzle Loading Rifle Association Championship Shoot in Friendship (August)

Daviess County Turkey Trot Festival (September)

Indianapolis 500

October–December

Parke County Covered Bridge Festival in Rockville (October)

Harvest Homecoming in New Albany (October)

Traditional Christmas at the Conner Prairie Pioneer Settlement (November and December)

Indianapolis Christmas Lighting Ceremony (November and December)

Indiana Day across the state (December 11)

Famous People

George Ade (1866–1944)	Humorist and playwright
Larry Bird (1956–)	Basketball player
Hoagland Howard (Hoagy) Carmichael (1899–1981)	Songwriter
Theodore Dreiser (1871–1945)	Author
Edward Eggleston (1837–1902)	Author and historian
Wilbur Charles (Weeb) Ewbank (1907–1998)	Football coach
John Milton Hay (1838–1905)	Diplomat and author
James (Jimmy) Riddle Hoffa (1913–1975?)	Labor leader
Michael Jackson (1958–)	Singer, dancer, songwriter
David Letterman (1944–)	Television host
Thomas Riley Marshall (1854–1925)	U.S. vice president
Jane Pauley (1950–)	Television journalist
Cole Albert Porter (1891–1964)	Lyricist and composer
Gene Stratton Porter (1868–1924)	Author
James Danforth Quayle (1947–)	U.S. vice president
James Whitcomb Riley (1849–1916)	Poet

David Letterman

Edd Roush (1893–1988)	Baseball player
Newton Booth Tarkington (1869–1946)	Author
Twyla Tharp (1941–)	Dancer and choreographer
Kurt Vonnegut (1922–)	Author
Lewis (Lew) Wallace (1827–1905)	U.S. general, diplomat, and author
Jessamyn West (1907–1984)	Author
Wendell L. Willkie (1892–1944)	Industrialist and political leader
Wilbur Wright (1867–1912)	Inventor and pioneer aviator

Twyla Tharp

To Find Out More

History

- Chambers, Catherine E., and John Lawn (illustrator). *Indiana Days: Life in a Frontier Town.* Mahwah, N.J.: Troll, 1999.

- Fradin, Dennis Brindell. *Indiana.* Chicago: Childrens Press, 1994.

- Swain, Gwenyth. *Indiana.* Minneapolis, Minn.: Lerner Publications Company, 1997.

- Thompson, Kathleen. *Indiana.* Austin, Tex.: Raintree/Steck Vaughn, 1996.

Biography

- Dolan, Sean. *Larry Bird.* Broomall, Penn.: Chelsea House, 1994.

- Fitz-Gerald, Christine Maloney. *William Henry Harrison: Ninth President of the United States.* Chicago: Childrens Press, 1987.

- Nicholson, Lois P. *Michael Jackson.* Broomall, Penn.: Chelsea House, 1994.

Fiction

- Bradley, Kimberly Brubaker, and David Kramer (illustrator). *Ruthie's Gift.* New York: Bantam Doubleday Dell, 1998.

- Wyman, Andrea. *Red Sky at Morning.* New York: Holiday House, 1991.

Websites

■ **Access Indiana Information Network**
http://www.state.in.us
The official website for the state

■ **The City of Indianapolis and Marion County**
http://www.indygov.org/
For information on Indiana's capital city

■ **Indiana State Library**
http://www.statelib.lib.in.us
For information on collections, databases, and other libraries

Addresses

■ **Auburn-Cord-Duesenberg Museum**
1600 South Wayne Street
P.O. Box 271
Auburn, IN 46706
To find out about the museum and tour, which feature the classic car

■ **The College Football Hall of Fame**
111 South St. Joseph Street
South Bend, IN 46601
To find information on the museum and the history of college football

■ **Indiana Department of Commerce**
Tourism and Marketing
  Division
One North Capitol
Suite 700
Indianapolis, IN 46204-2288
For information on recreation in the state

■ **Secretary of State's Office**
State House
Room 201
Indianapolis, IN 46204
For information on the history of Indiana

Index

Page numbers in *italics* indicate illustrations.

Meet the
Author

Ann Heinrichs fell in love with faraway places while reading Doctor Dolittle books as a child. She has traveled through most of the United States and several countries in Europe, as well as North and West Africa, the Middle East, and East Asia. She first got to know Indiana when she lived there for four years, and she has been back to visit many times.

"Trips are fun, but the real work—tracking down all the factual information for a book—begins at the library. I head straight for the reference department. Some of my favorite resources are statistical abstracts and the library's computer databases.

"For this book, I also read local newspapers from several Indiana cities. The Internet was a super research tool, too. The state home page and the state library and historical websites are chock-full of information.

"To me, writing nonfiction is a bigger challenge than writing fiction. With nonfiction, you can't just dream something up—everything has to be true. When I uncover the facts, they always turn out to be more spectacular than fiction could ever be."

Ann Heinrichs grew up in Fort Smith, Arkansas, and now lives in Chicago. She is the author of more than thirty books for children and young adults on American, Asian, and African history and culture. Several of her books have received state and national awards.

Ms. Heinrichs has also written numerous newspaper, magazine, and encyclopedia articles and critical reviews. As an advertising copywriter, she has covered everything from plumbing hardware to Oriental rugs and porcelain dolls. She holds a bachelor's and master's degree in piano performance. These days, her performing arts are t'ai chi chuan and kung fu sword.

Photo Credits

Photographs ©:

AllSport USA: 122 (Andy Lyons), 123 (David Seelig), 7 top right, 119, 133 (David Taylor)

AP/Wide World Photos: 121, 131 bottom (Michael Conroy), 87 top, 113, 114 top, 116, 117, 134

Clint Farlinger: 58

Corbis-Bettmann: 90 (George Bridges)

Courtesy Secretary of State Office: 84 top

Dembinsky Photo Assoc.: 6 bottom, 61 (Stan Osolinski)

Envision: 95 (Steven Needham)

Folio, Inc.: 91 (Michael Patrick)

H. Armstrong Roberts, Inc.: 81 (W. J. Scott)

Indiana State Library: 29 bottom, 39

International Stock Photo: 105 (Andre Jenny)

James P. Rowan: 15, 70, 85 bottom, 129 top

Kent and Donna Dannen: 7 bottom, 75, 85 top, 130

Liaison Agency, Inc.: 29 top, 32, 43, 115 top, 125 (Hulton Getty), 114 bottom, 135 (Don Perdue)

Marilyn Nenni: 94

Mary and John Eicher: 74, 100, 107

New England Stock Photo: 66 (Cheryl A. Ertelt), 7 top center, 51 (Jeff Greenberg)

North Wind Picture Archives: 9, 10, 17, 18, 19, 21, 24, 27, 28, 30, 31, 33, 36, 115 bottom

Rich Clark: cover, back cover, 2, 6 top left, 7 top left, 38, 49, 52, 62, 63, 64, 65, 67, 73, 76, 77, 78, 83, 84 bottom, 92, 93, 97, 106, 110, 118, 128 bottom, 129 bottom, 131 top, 132, 133 top

Richard Fields: 12, 13, 55, 56, 59, 87 bottom, 102, 103, 112

Stock Montage, Inc.: 14, 23, 35, 37, 41, 42

The Northern Indiana Historical Society: 44, 45

Tom Stack & Associates: 6 top center, 47, 50, 69 (Sharon Gerig)

Tom Till: 8, 54

Tony Stone Images: 82, 128 top (Cathlyn Melloan)

Unicorn Stock Photos: 6 top right, 80 (Tom Edwards), 71, 109 (Jeff Greenberg), 26 (Charles E. Schmidt)

University of Notre Dame, Sports Information Department: 124

William Harter: 48, 99, 101

Maps by XNR Productions, Inc.